READ
TO WRITE

READ TO WRITE

*Using Children's Literature
as a Springboard
to Writing*

JOHN WARREN STEWIG

HAWTHORN BOOKS, INC.
Publishers / NEW YORK

Grateful acknowledgment is made for permission to quote from copyrighted material: "Forsythia" reprinted from *Concrete Poetry: A World View,* edited by Mary Ellen Solt, copyright © 1970 by Indiana University Press, Bloomington, Indiana, by permission of the publisher; "March" from *A Child's Calendar* by John Updike, illustrated by Nancy Burkert, copyright © 1965, published by Alfred A. Knopf, Inc.; "A Modern Dragon" from *Songs From Around a Toadstool Table,* copyright © 1967 by Rowena Bennett, previous copyright © 1937, 1930 by Follett Publishing Company, used by permission of Follett Publishing Company, a division of Follett Corporation; "Patience and Concomdure" from *Words Words Words* by Mary O'Neill, copyright © 1966, published by Doubleday & Company, Inc.

READ TO WRITE

Library of Congress Catalog Card Number: 74-20291.

ISBN: 0-8015-4586-2

10 9 8 7 6 5 4 3 2 1

To Jack,
with appreciation for showing me
how to learn about language

CONTENTS

PREFACE

Most of us write each day. Often our writing is simple: a list, or a note to remind ourselves to do something. Sometimes it is more difficult, perhaps a letter of condolence. A few of us put words together to make a living.

Regardless of the nature of the writing we do, we probably share two things in common. First, we seldom or never think consciously of the process or act of writing. Second, we rarely consider how we learned to write and the ease or difficulty with which we mastered the skills of writing.

Yet, by considering these two aspects, we may gain insights into effective ways of helping children write. Being concerned with this problem, I looked to these two aspects for clues to the potential nature of a writing curriculum for young children. What follows is a description of a writing program designed to help children think consciously about the nature of the writing process in order to improve their ability to express ideas in written words.

I want to thank the group of teachers listed below for their cooperation in testing this composition program with their children. Without their help the program would not have been developed or this description of it written. Those who helped with the program were:

Marion Block	Joan Groth
Carol Buchman	Mary Kling
Lois Campbell	Carol Krahn
Rita Dufner	Barbara Pueringer
Barbara Franczyk	Helen Smith
Jean Gardner	Betty Thwaits
Jody Goral	Cindy Young

Never having worked with any of these teachers before, I had some trepidation about asking them to launch a full-scale experimental program. They accepted the challenge graciously and with enthusiasm. Their interest sustained me throughout the year we worked together.

The results are included here. As you will recognize, the children's writing included represents only a small portion of the total year's compositions. In an effort to include the work of many children we sometimes purposely eliminated an excellent story or poem if that child's work was already included. Thus we feel that while the samples included are selected, they are also representative.

The teachers who experimented with this program responded enthusiastically; they and their children enjoyed it. More importantly, the teachers felt that the program did indeed result in increased writing skills. They report that the writing the children did was more effective as a result.

As you read about the program and enjoy the children's writing, perhaps you will become interested in trying it with your children. I am convinced the program has potential for helping young people become better writers. I hope you will try it with your children and share the results with me and with other teachers, librarians, and parents.

1

CHILDREN
AND WRITING

A little boy sits at a table, firmly clutching a large wooden pencil as he makes ungainly scrawls unintelligible to anyone but a doting parent or a perceptive teacher. His face mirroring his concentration, his entire being is focused on translating an idea into those scrawls an adult has told him are called words. From this young child's efforts at expression to the fluid phrases arranged with care by an adult writer is a long, often difficult road. While few children in school will ever choose to devote the years necessary to the task of becoming a professional writer, schools are nonetheless interested in helping all children develop writing competency. One of the school's goals is to aid children in becoming able to express their ideas fluently, whether in the form of a poem, a story, a descriptive paragraph, a report, or a letter. How the school has done this and alternate ways the school could do this are the major concerns of this book. To begin, it is important to consider the types of writing children are asked to do.

11

TYPES OF WRITING

To be neutral about the term *creativity* today is near heresy, for it ranks in importance with other educational shibboleths. One must be in favor of the term or risk being out of step. Bearing this danger in mind, I should like to consider the term *creative writing* and then discard it.

Definitions of creativity are rampant, and reading several of them will give a many-faceted understanding of an elusive term.[1] In relation to writing, the term *creative* is commonly used to refer to a particular type of writing. Descriptions of the writing elementary school children are asked to do generally contrast two terms: *creative writing* and *practical writing*. This dichotomy, like many others, is artificial. *Creative writing* is usually described as the stories and poems children write that flow from ideas and inspirations uniquely their own, and in which they are motivated by the teacher to express their feelings, thoughts, and emotions about a topic. In such writing children are often encouraged to concentrate on getting all their ideas out on the paper with little regard for conventional forms and the mechanics of writing, because the content is what is valued.

In contrast, the term *practical writing* is used to suggest more formal writing, done with a reader in mind, in which certain mechanical amenities are observed. Letters and reports are among the kinds of expository writing included in this category. It should be obvious, of course, that practical writing needs creativity to bring it to life. Individuality and uniqueness can make the letter form, for instance, a challenge to the writer and a delight to the reader. It can be argued that any good piece of practical writing should contain elements of creativity, and that any piece of creative writing

[1] Among the many books available, you might find the following helpful: Frank X. Barron. *Creative Person and Creative Process;* Stanley Rosner, *The Creative Experience;* Hugh Lytton, *Creativity and Education.*

must include some minimal attention to practical considerations.

Such divisions do not seem conducive to getting at the real problem of how to improve writing ability. So, for the purposes of this book, the assumption will be made that any writing a child does is creative. Some writing may be much more creative than other writing, but when a child struggles to put ideas on paper—whether it be a story, a letter, a report, or a poem—he or she is being creative.

WRITING IN THE CURRICULUM

Many elementary curricula make provisions for composition. Children are provided with a variety of experiences designed to motivate them to write. This happens in kindergarten when a teacher draws children together after a trip to a fire station and encourages them to dictate their reactions to the experience. It also happens in sixth grade when a teacher may use a film, or perhaps a picture, to encourage children to compose in writing their individual reactions to the stimuli. In between, children encounter many different motivations to write. There are a wide variety of materials available to help a teacher who wants to plan writing experiences for children.[2]

It is interesting that, though most children do write as part of the elementary language-arts program, it is only rarely that they are asked to reflect upon the act of composition itself. In typical programs children express themselves when doing creative writing, and they give careful attention to such mechanical considerations as punctuation and spelling when they are doing practical writing. It is

[2] Among the many fine materials available are: Richard Corbin, *The Teaching of Writing in Our Schools;* Walter T. Petty and Mary E. Bowen, *Slithery Snakes and Other Aids to Children's Writing;* Grace Pratt-Butler, *Let Them Write Creatively.*

only rarely that much attention is given to helping them shape and reshape their writing to make it more effective. Conscious thought about the process of composing is seldom a part of elementary writing programs. The purpose of this book is to point out how children can consciously examine the composition process and experience a set of writing problems designed to improve their ability to write.

HOW CREATIVE WRITING GOT THAT WAY

Little attention was paid to young children's ability to write creatively until a group of educators, since then labeled "progressive," appeared on the American educational scene. From the time schools were begun in this country until early in the 1900s, great care was given to mastery of correct forms, punctuation and spelling rules were rigorously taught and practiced, and children spent time copying prose and poetry other people had written. But little time was devoted to developing children's ability to express themselves fluently.

Beginning in the early 1920s, several educational leaders looked to new approaches, designed to draw out children's potential and build upon it, rather than relying on children's ability to absorb quantities of facts. The educational literature from this period is perhaps most striking because of the similarities between ideas advanced then and those currently in vogue. Several writers turned their attention specifically to children's communication skills.

One of these was Hughes Mearns, and his book was to prove the beginning of an approach to children's writing that has attracted a wide following.[3] The book provided a rationale for including writing in the elementary curriculum and was full of examples of students' writing. It provided

[3] Hughes Mearns, *Creative Power.* Originally published in 1929, the book is still in print and merits reading. It is a fresh, convincing statement of the abilities of children in many creative endeavors.

much encouragement to adventuresome teachers willing to try a new and relatively untested way of working with children.

Since the publication of Mearns's book, instruction in creative writing has followed, in the main, one philosophical direction, as expressed in the writing of such authors as Applegate, Burrows, and others. In a slight oversimplification, this philosophical base states that:

- All children can write creatively.
- A supportive atmosphere and topics are the two main ingredients that the teacher supplies.
- Little or no emphasis on correctness or editing is necessary. Acceptance is most important.

REASONS FOR WRITING IN THE CURRICULUM

In addition to revealing an identifiable philosophical base, a review of the literature about children's writing indicates that there are several reasons advanced for including writing experiences in the curriculum. Among the most commonly mentioned are:

- Experiences with creative writing lead to a *free expression* of the child's ideas. In creative writing sessions children are encouraged to take an idea or ideas uniquely their own and weave them into an individual expression.[4]
- The process of writing itself provides a *catharsis*, a release from the tensions of other areas in the curriculum. The writing experience lets children

[4] A typical statement of this value is included in James A. Smith, *Creative Teaching of the Language Arts in the Elementary School.*

express their feelings and emotions about topics they feel too deeply about to discuss.[5]

- A value to the teacher is that the products of the writing period give *insights into the needs and problems* of the child.[6]
- Another reason for including writing in the curriculum is to provide children with a means of communicating their ideas and reactions to others in a *permanent form*.[7]
- A final reason advanced for including writing in the curriculum is to produce more capable writers and more competent writing. Of the five reasons this is probably the one least frequently mentioned by experts.

Certainly it is difficult to argue against any of these reasons for planning writing experiences for young children. Yet, analysis reveals that only one of these is a unique justification for a writing program: the production of better writers and writing. Other areas in the school curriculum can claim to advance all four of the other purposes. For example, art and music programs are often better able to promote the free expression of ideas than is the writing program. The presence of counselors in elementary schools offers more direct access to children's needs and problems with less danger of misinterpretation. Finally, creative dramatics allows for catharsis more effectively, because children can say and act out what they feel under the guise of characters they have assumed, without the attendant problems of mastery of the mechanical skills necessary for writing.

[5] A statement about this reason is included in Walter T. Petty et al., *Experiences in Language*, p. 279.

[6] This idea is expressed in Ruth G. Strickland, *The Language Arts in the Elementary School*, pp. 299–324.

[7] Mildred R. Donoghue, *The Child and the English Language Arts*, p. 204.

Therefore, it appears that the only goal unique to a writing program, and as a result, the most important one, is to produce better writers and writing.

RESULTS OF CURRENT WRITING CURRICULA

Several generations of schoolchildren have experienced to greater or lesser degrees such writing programs as the one described above. The problem is that too little concrete evidence exists that such programs produce an important result: better writers and writing. There is, among authorities on creative writing, a nearly unanimous reluctance to evaluate the writing done by children. In fact, some authorities warn against such evaluation. Much anecdotal information is available about the creativity expressed by children who have written in the freeing environment recommended. Despite the interesting and engrossing nature of this material, there is little empirical information to show that the writing children do at the end of six years of elementary school is better *as a result of writing programs* than it would have been simply as a result of maturity.

It can be argued that many collections of children's writing have been published containing exceptionally original writing. It is also true that such collections are, in the main, highly selective. The works finally included are only a small body of writing lifted from a much larger mass of work of indeterminate quality. Some, though not most, experts on writing have included several samples from the same child. These samples do show freedom of expression, some charming insights into life, and the ability to coin an original phrase or figure of speech. Any extended analysis of improvement or maturity, however, as a result of the writing program, is nonexistent.

A POTENTIAL AUDIENCE

Do children who experience a writing program based on creativity as the most crucial element turn out to be better writers than other children? Results are, at best, equivocal. Teachers who have tried this approach generally seem enthusiastic about it, though others who read what students write have expressed doubts. The comments of high school teachers, college professors, and other adults indicate concern over the degree of writing skill acquired. Though many students have experienced a writing program, it seems that few can write well. Typical of those who are dubious about current approaches is Evans,[8] who comments on the

> imprecision in word and idea, incoherence of structure and argument, the almost compulsive injection of wholly irrelevant personal attitudes into every piece of writing the student does.

He sees the reason for this as

> a mistaken emphasis on "self-expression" and "imaginative" writing, to the virtual exclusion of guided exercises, however elementary, in such forms as objective description, comparison, contrast, definition, and explanation.

The problem, he continues, is that the child has

> not [been] shown how to construct a simple plot, or create a character, or write interesting dialogue, not

[8] Robert Evans, "A Glove Thrown Down," *Elementary English*, May 1967. pp. 523–27. The author points out the fallacy of assuming that children can write significant prose without direct instruction and makes a convincing argument for structuring beginning writing experiences around careful observation of objects.

led, in short, to an early awareness that all writing
needs direction and control. . . .

Evans is not alone in wondering if current approaches to
writing instruction develop children's potential to its fullest.[9]

A NEW APPROACH

The question must be raised: Would another approach to
the teaching of writing lead to the goal identified earlier—
better writers and writing? The approach to writing described
in this book is in some ways quite different than the approach
commonly used in elementary schools now. Is it better?
There is some initial informal evidence that it is, and many
samples of children's works are included in the book to
demonstrate the quality of writing done by children exposed
to this approach. This approach is, however, quite new. It
has been tested by the teachers acknowledged in the preface,
but it needs to be further tested by many other teachers. In
addition, it needs testing over a period of years to determine
if in fact children who experience such a program are better
writers at the end of elementary school than children who
did not participate. Such implementation and research will
take several years. For now it is my intent to present this
approach so convincingly that you will want to try it with
your children.

The fundamental assumption on which this program rests
is that writing is a skill. Skills can be learned and, after
being learned, they can be improved. Children you work
with, at whatever level, will possess composing skills. The
composing skills of young children will be oral. The

[9] An example of this concern is seen in Raymond Fournier, *Thinking and
Writing*. The series attempts to develop in children the skills of selecting,
organizing, and presenting information. It leads a child through five different
levels of increasingly complex problems designed to develop these skills.

composing skills of older children will also include writing. Your job is to further develop and expand upon the skills already possessed by your students. A major task of this book is to point out ways in which you may further develop the writing, or composing, skills of your students.

This assumption does not negate the importance of self-expression or creativity. Certainly no sensitive and perceptive teacher will consciously thwart a child's individuality and self-expression. The question is one of emphasis. In this program developing writing ´skills is seen as more crucial than the encouragement of self-expression. The program does not deny the emotional values that can come from the writing process, or the importance of the school respecting and enhancing the child's self-concept and creativity. Rather, the program simply emphasizes the cognitive and skill development as more important in this particular segment of the general elementary curriculum.

HOW ARE SKILLS DEVELOPED?

The program uses a recommended set of examples drawn from the wide range of literature for children as the basis for writing sessions.[10] The reasons for this are:

- If children know and understand good literature, there is the opportunity for them to transfer something of what they know into what they write.
- If children are immersed in literature and encouraged to talk about it, reflect upon it, argue

[10] It must be emphasized that the books named are *recommended*. From the wealth of literature available any teacher can select other, equally useful selections to share with children, once he or she understands how the writing program works.

about it, and raise questions about it, there is the chance they may become better writers by using literature as models on which to build.

• There is some indication that children, especially those in the intermediate grades, write more effectively as a result of vicarious experiences. One author reports that these children seem to turn from first-hand experiences as a motivation for writing to respond to less immediate motivations.[11]

The foundation of the program is a rich, constant experience with literature continuing throughout the entire elementary school years. Children are encouraged to think consciously about what they read, to speculate upon the nature of the literature, and to hypothesize about the writers' purposes in writing as they did. This program does not ask children to just passively absorb and "appreciate" but rather to interact with the literature selections that the teacher presents.

THE IMPORTANCE OF LITERATURE

It is probably true that most elementary school teachers understand the values that accrue as a result of sharing literature with children. Many teachers share books with their children in an informal period sometime during the day. In most situations, however, this sharing is somewhat unplanned. One writer has commented that, while there is

[11] Neal R. Edmund, "Do Intermediate Grade Pupils Write About Their Problems?" *Elementary English*, 37 (1960): 242–43. The author reports that children wrote longer stories, using more descriptive words, when motivations, including the use of literature, were vicarious.

a wealth of literature for children, there is a dearth of planned sequential programs of literature designed to acquaint children with the range of styles, genres, topics, and approaches.[12]

Since the first component, or strand, of this writing program is literature input, it is imperative that teachers be well acquainted with children's literature in all its forms, so that what they select to share will advance the goals of the writing program. Teachers who are familiar with all types of literature, as well as with the specific goals of this program, can choose books that will be both enjoyable and also an asset in helping children improve their writing.

An intensive experience with literature is crucial to the success of this program. It is important that the teacher reads to the children every day. This means not only at the primary grade level, where the practice is fairly common, but also at the intermediate level, where it is less common. Twenty minutes per day spent reading to the children will result in better writing as the children unconsciously assimilate aspects of what they are hearing. As one writer has said:

> Teachers who read to boys and girls . . . will, in the process, expose them to the full beauty and flavor of the English language. . . . Indeed, children often recognize immediately a particularly melodious, rhythmic or emotional word or phrase . . . and thousands of . . . such language elements have been memorized instantly by children.[13]

In describing the literature input provided for children by teachers in the British Infant Schools, another author describes for us justification for the sharing recommended here:

[12] Norine Odland, *Teaching Literature in the Elementary School.*
[13] Robert Whitehead, *Children's Literature,* p. 81.

Reading to children not only stimulates thought and brings forms of literature to children they might not ordinarily read . . . but . . . it also helps improve writing style through hearing the vocabulary, sentence construction, grammar and syntactical arrangements, organization and approach used by other writers.[14]

TREATMENT OF LITERATURE

The fact that this writing program is based on literature does not mean that teachers should attempt to dissect what they read with the children, belaboring aspects of construction, style, figurative language, and vocabulary choice. Indeed, this would spoil the chance for children to appreciate the literature they are hearing. Some of the literature will be discussed; other selections will simply be read and enjoyed. Still other literature will later be used consciously as a basis for specific writing experiences. But in leading any discussion the teacher keeps in mind the need to draw out from children their reactions to what they read rather than consciously implant in their minds large amounts of cognitive information. He or she may start informally with very young children:

- What part of the story did you like best? Can you tell us why?
- Which part was most exciting or interesting?
- Which of the people in the story did you like best? Can you tell us why?

Later, the questions become more complex:

[14] Howard E. Blake, "Written Composition in English Primary Schools," *Elementary English,* October 1971, pp. 605–16.

- Why do you think we don't like that character?
  What does he or she do that makes us feel that
  way?
- Why do you think the story happened where the
  author made it happen?
- That's an interesting word. Why do you think
  the author chose to use it instead of another one?

Older children deal with questions at a quite sophisticated
level:

- What do you notice about the differences in the
  language the characters speak?
- How did the author convey the relationship between the characters without simply telling us?
- What reasons might there be for the character to
  act that way?

In all discussion sessions the teacher works diligently to
instill and reinforce the idea that there is no one right
answer to such questions as these. It is important that
children see literature as open to a variety of interpreta-
tions; their answers to the questions must be encouraged,
even if they are not the ones the teacher would have given.
The purpose of such discussion sessions is to encourage children to speculate about the literature and about the author's
reasons for writing in a particular way. Perhaps in some cases
we can come close to a finite, correct answer. In other instances, answers will remain speculation. This is fine. What
the teacher is doing is encouraging children to think deeply,
and to reflect upon and wonder about what has been read
to them.

The above is not to suggest that discussion follows the
reading every day. This would be a mistake. There are times
with some selections when the teacher simply allows what

has been read to sink into the child's unconscious mind, allows children to privately mull over their own reactions to and questions about what they have heard. No attempt is made to fix the material, to arrive at a consensus, or to have children remember what they have read. One author has called this *impressional treatment*.[15] The idea in this approach is that each child will take from the experience whatever is relevant to him or her. What is taken in such a situation cannot, and should not be measured. Each child will, in fact, take something from the reading. There is no particular reason for the teacher to know precisely what each child gets from the experience.

In planning the reading, teachers should balance the two approaches. Too much conscious discussion may well result in diminishing interest; too little will result in a lessened impact on the writing children will do. The balance is crucial, but it cannot be prescribed. Teachers interested in trying this writing program with their children will need to develop their own sensitivity to deciding which pieces of literature should be discussed and how extensive the discussion should be.

CHILDREN AS READERS

In addition to being provided input by the teacher, the children should be encouraged to read widely. They must be encouraged to read to themselves, to their peers, and to younger children. Again, such reading must take place every day if the benefits are to be seen in the writing children do. It must be pointed out that this reading is not the kind done in reading instruction classes, but rather free reading of any books the children find interesting.

It is important that children read what other children

15 David C. Davis et al., *Playway*, pp. 19–21.

—not just adult authors—have written. Sharing following the writing sessions is of course essential, but the teacher must seek other sources of children's writing. There are now available many collections of children's writing.[16] These should be made available to children, and it is important to point out that the authors were other children. This is necessary to establish the understanding that writing is a legitimate activity for children and that reading what other children have written can be interesting and informative. Teachers implementing this writing program should make concerted efforts to get samples of children's writing from other teachers in addition to published collections. Always be sure to check with teachers in your building or other schools in your district, and share samples of writing back and forth.

The purpose of all this reading of literature, including stories and poetry written by children, is to help children see that reading and writing are closely linked. The reading of literature and the writing of it are thus seen as inter-related processes. This overcomes the idea that too often exists in children's minds that literature is something written by adults.

OBSERVATION SKILLS

In addition to the input provided when the teacher shares literature, this program emphasizes observation leading to writing. To develop writing skills, teachers will often involve children in a two-step process of observing something in their environment and then writing about it. This is important, as

[16] Mauree Applegate, *When the Teacher Says, "Write a Story"* contains many stories to share with children. English children's writing is included in Margaret Langdon, *Let the Children Write*. A subscription to *Kids* Magazine provides a steady supply of children's writing (subscription information: Kids' Publishers, Inc., Box 30, Cambridge, Mass., 02139).

most adult writers are keen observers. They observe the world around them, taking in the elements in their environments, and then shape and reshape what they have seen so it can be used in their writing. Similarly, children should be encouraged to develop that skill in observing and then to describe in telling fashion what they have observed; and this will help improve their writing. This observation might be of some object in their classroom or of the way in which a person talks or moves. In either case, keen observation and then exploring ways to describe what was observed are important. Searching for exactly the right words to tell a reader about what was observed is problem solving of the highest level.[17]

WRITING ASSIGNMENTS BASED ON LITERATURE

The third component of this writing program is a set of writing exercises, or problems, which are directly based upon literature selections. The input literature, mentioned earlier, is for impressional purposes, and does not immediately affect the children's writing. However, this component, or strand, of the program makes direct use of some piece of literature. A story is presented to children for the express purpose of serving as motivational material about which children will write. The material might be selected as a base for a characterization problem or as background for an experience in some aspect of plot creation, for example. The relationship between literature and the children's own writing is more direct in this strand of the program than in the input strand discussed earlier.

[17] It should be emphasized here that the word *right* is not synonymous with *correct*. What we are talking about has nothing to do with correctness in either a grammatical or a mechanical sense. What we are talking about is helping children understand the joy that can come from finally thinking of exactly the right word to put into print—the essence of the idea they want to share.

THE EDITING COMPONENT

Unlike some other programs of composition instruction, this one emphasizes having children edit their work after the initial writing is complete. What is *editing* and how do children learn editing skills?

There are two kinds of editing; the second is of concern to the teacher. The first is *concurrent editing.* That is, in the process of composing, we all make selections of words and ideas as we get thoughts on paper. This is often a very intuitive process—so intuitive that we may not be consciously aware we are doing it. As we think of a sentence in our mind before writing it down, we choose the word *maroon,* for example, instead of *red.* It more accurately expresses our idea, so we edit out *red* and substitute *maroon.* In composing a paragraph, we think of many possible sentences and choose from among these the ones we want to include. This we have called concurrent editing, done during the process of writing. Because it is an active, often subconscious, internal process, and because teachers cannot oversee the process in entire classrooms of individuals, there is little help they can offer with this kind of editing.

In contrast, the second type is called *completion editing* because it is a necessary step to bring the writing to a finished state. That is, after the first initial creative impulse that results in a piece of writing, both the child and the teacher can contemplate what has been written. Because the ideas are manifested—caught, if you will—in writing, children can look at what they have written. This is the stage at which they can look again at those choices they made while writing. The children can examine their writing and, if taught how, can edit their own work, bringing it to completion. Carefully they can examine the ideas, their interrelation to each other, their sequence, word choices, emphasis, and other elements and analyze how closely the writing came to representing their ideas.

It is at this stage that children reshape their writing to say more effectively what they want to say. It is at this point in the writing process that children can change, add to, relocate, or delete parts of their writing to make it more satisfying to them.

Two other statements help define this process:

- The key concept in the above paragraph is children changing their work to make it more satisfying to *them*. It is not a case of the teacher telling children what they must do to meet the teacher's standards for writing. The children must understand editing as a process that individuals engage in to make their writing more closely mirror their own thoughts. While the teacher certainly does guide children to think about aspects of their composition as they edit, he or she does not enforce his or her own ideas of what should be done in a composition.

- The term *editing* refers *only* to content changes children make in their writing. It has nothing to do with mechanical correctness in such items as spelling, capitalization, punctuation, or handwriting. These are important, of course, but are called *correcting*. The two processes must be kept separate. How to handle correcting is left up to the individual teacher. The focus in this book will be on helping children develop editing skills. Further attention is given to the distinction between these two terms and to how to help children edit in chapter eight.

SUMMARY

Developing elementary school children's composition skills is not an easy task. But it can be a rewarding one for both teacher and students. One reason why teaching writing is difficult is that writing skills are acquired slowly, over an extended period of time. Another reason is that sequential, organized composition programs designed to help children learn writing skills are rare. This program makes a beginning attempt to develop such a program. The program described here is based on four components:

- intensive literature input
- writing assignments based on observations
- writing assignments based on literature
- editing as a means of improving compositions

Each of these components are strands that recur throughout the following chapters.

2

WRITING
WITH AND FOR
THE VERY YOUNG

Three components form the base for this writing program: wide input reading, writing based on observation, and writing based on literature. The advantages of wide reading were described in the previous chapter. With the very young child, preschool through first or second grade, the reading must be done by the teacher. Nevertheless, the advantages still accrue.

- The children enjoy listening to a teacher who has prepared the reading material well.
- The experience of listening to literature for pleasure provides a good contrast with more academic areas of the curriculum.
- The reading period exposes children to a variety of writing they might not otherwise encounter.[1]

The advantages of oral sharing of literature have been pointed out by many authors. In addition, the sharing of

[1] Shelton L. Root, "What's Wrong with Reading Aloud?" *Elementary English*, December 1967, pp. 929–32. The author describes in wry fashion reasons why teachers read aloud only infrequently, and he considers the types of literature best shared aloud.

material in this way provides another advantage especially crucial to this writing program. The literature forms a foundation on which writing experiences will be built. What the children hear forms a source of ideas, an input to be assimilated and used as they wish.

PREWRITING EXPERIENCES

Before storywriting must come storytelling; we have ample research evidence that children need to attain oral fluency before attempting mastery of written forms. Children can best be shown the delights of storytelling by example. A teacher who is an exiting storyteller, armed with a wide variety of tales to tell, can easily encourage children to tell stories. What qualities are necessary to be an effective storyteller?

The teacher interested in becoming an effective storyteller must:

- know a variety of stories to tell, ranging from old folktales to more modern tales.
- learn how to take a favorite story and adapt it for effective telling. Suggestions about how to do this are included in the following section.
- learn to use his or her voice effectively, to manipulate such elements as pitch, stress, juncture (pauses), volume, and tempo to hold the listeners' attention.

THE TEACHER AS STORYTELLER

There are two purposes in teachers telling stories to their children. *First,* the pure pleasure of listening to a well-told story is a joy for children, and in this rather hectic age a pleasure they may not experience other places than in school. *Second,* teachers are trying to establish in children's minds that this oral activity is worth the time and concern of adults. Their final goal is to motivate children so they will want to tell stories to the group. How do you accomplish this goal?

The first step is to choose a story which you like: one which captures your imagination and to which you will be willing to devote some amount of time. I often find it helpful to simply read half a dozen stories and then put the books aside for a week or so. After that time, the one which returns to my mind is probably the one worth learning.

In preparing the story for telling, there are three basic steps. First, you must divide the story into *units of action.* As you read most stories, you will notice that they seem to divide into an easily definable set of actions, or episodes. These can be summarized in note form, and then the sequence of these units of action can be learned. This procedure is, for most people, a more efficient way of learning a story than simply trying to begin at the beginning and memorize it.

The procedure of dividing a story into units of action can be illustrated by using the old tale, "Snowdrop," by Grimm.[2]

Unit One

A very brief scene sets the stage for what will follow. The good queen, seated at a window in winter, wishes for a

[2] You might choose to use *Grimm's Fairy Tales,* illustrated by Arthur Rackham. Though the original edition has been out of print for some time, a new edition with full-color reproductions of Rackham's original artwork has been issued by Viking Press (1973). An equally charming version children will enjoy is *Snow-white and the Seven Dwarfs.* This edition features a translation by the poet Randall Jarrell and extraordinary illustrations by Nancy Ekholm Burkert. The double-page, full-color illustrations are full of authentic detail, rendered with precision and grace in a subtle palette.

daughter with skin white as snow, cheeks red as blood, and with hair as black as ebony. Her wish is granted; she has the child, Snowdrop, but dies in childbirth.

Unit Two

The new queen, proud and haughty, cannot bear that anyone be more beautiful than she is. In this unit she is consulting her magic mirror, which reconfirms her belief that she is the most beautiful.

Unit Three

Trouble develops, for as Snowdrop grows to be seven years old, her beauty rivals the queen's. In this unit the queen gets the unpleasant revelation from her mirror that Snowdrop is indeed more beautiful than she.

Unit Four

The queen dispatches the huntsman with Snowdrop and instructions about her murder.

Unit Five

In this forest scene the huntsman, full of pity for Snowdrop, sets her free. To provide the tokens demanded by the queen, he kills a fawn to obtain the lungs and liver that will satisfy the queen.

Unit Six

Snowdrop arrives at the house of the seven dwarfs. They are away, and she falls asleep. When they come back, they do not disturb her. The following morning, they make an agreement that she stay with them, keeping their house in return for her keep.

Unit Seven

The queen discovers from her mirror that the huntsman has deceived her: Snowdrop is still alive. She disguises herself, goes to the cottage, offering laces for sale. There she tricks Snowdrop, who had let her in in order to inspect the laces the Queen has. The Queen laces up Snowdrop, who falls down, appearing to be dead.

Unit Eight

The seven dwarfs return home. They see the problem, undo the laces, and Snowdrop is saved. They admonish her not to let anyone into the cottage.

Unit Nine

The queen discovers from her mirror that Snowdrop is still alive. She takes a poisoned comb, disguises herself, and returns to the cottage. Snowdrop is beguiled into letting her in. When the queen combs Snowdrop's hair, Snowdrop falls down as if dead.

Unit Ten

The seven dwarfs return home. They see the problem, remove the comb and Snowdrop is saved. They again admonish her not to let anyone into the cottage.

Unit Eleven

The queen discovers from her mirror that Snowdrop is still alive. She prepares a poisoned apple, disguises herself, and returns to the cottage. She tricks Snowdrop into eating the poisoned half of the apple by eating the unpoisoned half herself. Snowdrop falls down, appearing to be dead.

Unit Twelve

The seven dwarfs return home. They search in vain to discover the nature of the problem but cannot rouse Snowdrop. Mournfully they put her in a glass casket.

Unit Thirteen

Some time has passed since Snowdrop has been put into the casket. A prince is riding by, sees Snowdrop, and declares his love for her. He must have her; at first the dwarfs resist. Finally, seeing the nature of his feelings for her, they agree. The servants of the prince carry the casket, but they stumble and, in so doing, dislodge the piece of poisoned apple from her throat. Snowdrop recovers, and the marriage is planned.

Unit Fourteen

This is the wedding scene at the castle. The evil queen, possessed by a desire to see Snowdrop and yet not wanting to attend, finally gives in and goes. When there, they bring a pair of iron slippers heated red hot. She is forced to dance until she falls down dead. The prince and Snowdrop live happily ever after.

The second task is to identify those sections that do need to be memorized verbatim. These might be some distinctive words or some repeated phrases. For instance, in "Snowdrop" we would retain, or learn verbatim, the following interchange between the queen and her mirror:

Mirror, Mirror on the wall,
Who is fairest of us all?

Queen, thou art fairest here, I hold,
But Snowdrop over the fells,
Who with the seven Dwarfs dwells,
Is fairer still a thousandfold.

We retain such elements, exactly as they are given in the story, because to eliminate them is to destroy some of the essence of the story. Many folk or fairy tales include elements like these, but they will not be difficult to learn.

The task of memorizing a story in its entirety seems formidable day—most teachers simply feel they don't have time for such tasks. The pleasant thing about most stories is that they don't need to be memorized. Stories are often more interesting, to both the teller and the listener, if the teller learns the units of action in the story and allows the story to unfold in a slightly different way each time it is told. The third task, learning the units of action or the sequence of events in the story, is not difficult. I frequently jot them in order on note cards and look them over each time I have a few minutes to wait for something. Using this technique, it seldom takes longer than a few days to firmly fix the units in my memory.

The main purpose of telling stories to children is to encourage them to tell stories of their own. Teachers should often ask children if they have stories of their own which they would like to tell the class. A teacher should not be disappointed if these first tentative stories offered by children are pale variants of stories already told. Originality is not the main goal of these beginning experiences. Children need to be encouraged to be fluent storytellers, and the teacher should comment positively on each story offered by a child, until it is clearly established in the children's minds that storytelling is an activity that is rewarded in the class-room. In addition to encouraging children to tell stories, storytelling also develops understanding about the oral tradition in literature.

UNDERSTANDING THE ORAL TRADITION

As early as kindergarten, children can easily understand the idea that today stories are usually written down in books, while many years ago stories were simply told, handed down from teller to teller. It is important to develop the idea that oral stories existed long before people knew how to write, and that each teller made slight changes. This insight is helpful to children in understanding the process of story creation. Using a variety of folktales and discussing their similarities and differences is a useful experience. One might use the story of the Gingerbread Boy. Which version do you know?

> One version is "The Pancake," taken from a collection of Norse tales originally published in 1874, now included in *The Arbuthnot Anthology of Children's Literature.* The story describes the goody and her seven hungry bairns from whom the pancake escaped and how the pancake eludes a variety of animals until at last it meets its inevitable end on the snout of a swimming pig. An interesting feature is the rhyming names the pancake attaches to each animal it encounters, e.g., Henny Penny. These names form a cumulative refrain, which children will delight in saying with the teller.
>
> In *The Bun* by Marcia Brown, very sketchy illustrations by the author done in limited color

depict the forest environment in which the action of the tale is set. Much specific detail, like the hen wing sweeper and the sour cream in the bun, contribute to the Russian flavor of the version. A deaf fox brings the bun to a sad end.

Virginia Haviland includes still another version, "The Wee Bannock," in *Favorite Fairy Tales Told in Scotland*. (A bannock is a flat oatmeal or barley cake usually baked on a griddle.) In this version the bannock runs into people's houses; in each case it encounters a human, in contrast to other versions which feature animals. After eluding such people as a tailor, a weaver, a churner, a miller, and a smithy, the bannock, exhausted, creeps under a gorse bush to rest. That proves its undoing, for it cannot see the fox hole under the bush. Falling into the hole, it is devoured by the fox. Vocabulary in this version is particularly interesting; children meet such words as *breeks (britches), spindle, distaff, anvil,* and *peat.*

"The Gingerbread Boy," in Miriam Blanton Huber's *Story and Verse for Children,* is a very succinct version that originally appeared in *St. Nicholas,* a magazine for children published in the nineteenth century. In this version an old man and his wife, childless, allow the gingerbread boy to escape, only to encounter a barn full of threshers, a field full of mowers, a cow, and a pig. Again a ravenous fox brings the end of the story.

Barbara Ireson's *The Gingerbread Man* is illustrated with bold, somewhat raffish pictures that make effective use of heavy black line. There is much exaggeration and silhouette. The repeated refrain is different than the one in other versions.

The gingerbread man encounters a variety of tradespeople before meeting his usual end because of the fox at the river.

Ruth Sawyer's *Journey Cake, Ho!* is an extended version by a master storyteller and includes monochromatic pictures full of rural details. The contrasting personalities of the woman, man, and their bound-out boy, Johnny, are convincingly developed. Less fully personified is the journey cake, whose wanderings result in the eventual restoration of good fortune. The refrains are in rhyme and the ending quite different than in most versions. This version provides much opportunity for vocabulary development.

Sharing some of these versions with children and using them as a base for discussion can result in valuable writing experiences.[3]

One kindergarten teacher devised an initial writing experience that engages children in a process called *parallel plot construction*. To begin, this teacher uses several of the versions of the old folktale described above. She reads these to children on succeeding days, initiating informal discussion about the stories. Children are encouraged to tell which version they like best and why. They are further helped to note similarities and differences in the stories. After this preparation the children are asked to create their own version of the story. In a recent class the children decided to make the runaway a hamburger from a well-known national chain of drive-ins. The hamburger rolled out of the shop, eluded a policeman, a mailman, some shoppers, and a delivery man

---

[3] Another variant, more divergent from the original than those listed above, is Arlene Mosel, *The Funny Little Woman*. Pursuit of her runaway dumpling leads the woman into trouble with the oni (evil creatures who live beneath the earth), but the ending is happy.

before rolling into the school. There it avoided the principal, the secretary, and the janitor, while rolling down the hall. Unfortunately, it rolled into the kindergarten, and was there devoured by the children! The story, dictated with gusto to the teacher, is an example of parallel plot construction. That is, the children simply took the plot of the folktale, changed some of the details, and dictated their own version of the story. The teacher was pleased with this effort, as it represented an understanding of the variations possible within the oral tradition. It was also evidence of beginning steps toward fluent storytelling. Later individual children will be asked to make up their own versions of this tale or of others, and more direct help will be given in adding new details and altering or adapting characters or plot. The essential idea is to help children see that, if they wish, they can use an idea from a story in making up a story of their own.

Another group of kindergarten children borrowed some ideas from the story of "The Pancake," but enriched it considerably by adding other details and an unusual ending. They dictated the following story to their teacher after hearing "The Pancake."

> Roly Poly Pumpkin lived at a restaurant. It rolled off the counter and out the door. Todd's house was next door. It rolled into Todd's back yard. There was a hill. The wind made the pumpkin tip over. Now it rolled into Scott's yard. Scott found it and carved it into a face with a bone for a mouth. Scott lit it for Halloween. On Monday he put it out for the garbageman. The pumpkin rolled out into the street. And then the truck came and smashed it flat like a pancake. Spot the dog came by and found it in the street. He ate it, and that was the end of it.

Further development of this idea is included in chapter five.

USING OTHER TELLERS

In addition to telling stories themselves, teachers can choose and share storytelling records with children. There is a wide variety of these available now. Many poets and writers have recorded their own work.[4] Talented performers have recorded both prose and poetry.[5] These range from simple Mother Goose rhymes [6] to more complex poetry [7] suitable for older children, and from folktales [8] to longer prose.[9]

These records offer two advantages. They provide a *change of pace* from teacher presentation. No matter how skilled the teacher is in reading and telling stories, the program will be richer if children are exposed to different storytellers'

[4] See, for example, Carl Sandburg's *Rootabaga Stories* and *Poems for Children*, Caedmon Records (TC 1089 and 1124), made memorable by the author's distinctive voice and interpretation.

[5] See two by a master storyteller: *Ruth Sawyer, Storyteller*, Weston Woods (701–702), and *Joy to the World*, Weston Woods (707). A delightful version of Grahame's *The Wind in the Willows* is available from Pathways of Sound (POS 1022, 1026, 1029, and 1039).

[6] A version with rhymes set to music is entitled *Nursery and Mother Goose Songs* and is available from Bowmar Records, Inc. (B-115 LP).

[7] A fine group presentation is *Poetry Parade*, featuring David McCord, Harry Behn, Karla Kuskin, and Aileen Fischer reading their own works; it is available from Weston Woods (703–704).

[8] *The Three Little Pigs and Other Fairy Tales* Caedmon Records, (TC 1129), is a charming retelling by a master vocal interpreter, Boris Karloff. The record includes an unusual version of "The Three Bears." Another version worth sharing is *Grimm Fairy Tales*, Caedmon Records (TC 1062), read by Joseph Schildkraut. In addition to such well-known European folk-tales, teachers should also acquaint children with less well-known tales. *Folk Tales from West Africa* (FP 103) and *Folk Tales from Indonesia* (FP 102), available from Folkways Records, are typical of the fine examples of such material now available.

[9] For example, a fine edition of Carroll's *Alice in Wonderland*, read by Cyril Ritchard in his engaging and fey style, is available from Riverside Records (SDP 22). The record box includes a facsimile volume of the 1865 first edition of the book.

techniques and voices. Children listen to a teacher's voice for anywhere from two hours a day in nursery and kindergarten situations to as much as six hours a day in intermediate grades. Listening to a different voice provides a pleasant variety.

Children thus exposed to a variety of *voice qualities* have a valuable opportunity for studying language. At any age level children can be asked to listen carefully to a storyteller record, and in the discussion following they can tell how the voice sounds and how the reading makes them feel. Developing such describing abilities is important. These describing abilities are useful in developing oral fluency and will also be of use later in writing. Children should be encouraged to use any words they can think of to tell how the voice sounds. For instance, "It sounds old," or "It sounds like gravel," or "It sounds funny." None of these are particularly perceptive descriptions of voice quality, but they should be accepted as a base for more sophisticated describing later. With older children the teacher should provide experiences that stimulate discussion of aspects of oral expression, including pitch, stress, juncture (pauses), tempo, and volume. An example may serve to point out how this is done.

In using the recording of "There was a crooked man" [10] with a group of fourth grade children, the discussion began with the simple statement that the voice sounded "creepy." Further discussion led to the understanding that it was because of the restricted volume, the lowered pitch, and the manipulation of juncture that the effect was created. Children then practiced reading the nursery rhyme themselves, experimenting with verbal elements to see if they could make an ominous and effective reading of the rhyme.

[10] Cyril Ritchard et al., *Mother Goose*, Caedmon Records (TC 1091). Well over sixty rhymes—some old favorites, others lesser known, but all interpreted with insight and verve by three gifted artists. An aural delight for adults as well.

Such activities as these, which engage children in active use of oral language, form a base for the writing experiences that come later. A good deal of discussion, questioning, verbal interaction, and dictation of stories must precede actual written composition by children. To hurry this phase of the preparation, to condense it in an effort to involve children immediately in actual writing of stories, is a mistake. The time spent in these preliminary activities is justified in the increased written fluency apparent later.

MUCH WRITING

This writing program puts great emphasis on dictation of stories. The dictation of stories can continue with groups often well into the second grade and perhaps longer for individual children having trouble mastering the mechanics of handwriting. Since all of this involves a lot of teacher time, a very practical question occurs. How does the teacher provide opportunities for children to tell their thoughts before they have the ability to write them themselves?

One way to keep the flow of ideas going and to involve children in dictation is to make use of group stories. These may involve all the children in a class, perhaps at the completion of a field trip or after an experience with a classroom visitor. Then the teacher draws the children around the chart stand or chalkboard and records their ideas. At other times a small subgroup may dictate a story related to something of interest just to them. Perhaps one of the children at a table has brought an unusual rock to class. It may be of some interest to those children sitting at the same table, but of little or no interest to other children in the room. Noticing that the children at the table have continued to feel, look at, smell, and otherwise examine the rock during the day, the teacher may ask that group of children if they would like to dictate a story about the rock.

WRITING BASED ON OBSERVATION: FIELD EXPLORATION

A vital part of any educational program should be the excursions into the community that teachers plan for their students. Much can indeed go on within the classroom; yet, some things can only happen when the class goes into the community to learn. A major reason for planning field trips is the related writing or dictating experiences that result.

The teacher needs to be thoroughly familiar with the resources offered by the community in order to plan helpful field excursions. For a long time experts have recommended field trips: to the zoo, a farm, a fire station, or perhaps a supermarket. There is nothing wrong with such trips, but they do not exhaust the possibilities within the community. Valuable input of language and vocabulary and a stimulating experience that challenges children to think, talk, and then dictate a written account results when the teacher plans more unusual experiences than those mentioned above.

Field exploration might include such *cultural experiences* as observing the rehearsal of a musical group, visiting an artist's studio, or taking a trip to a museum. Field exploration might include contact with *professional aspects* of the community as provided by a visit to a lawyer's office, to a hospital, or to an architect's office. Field exploration can also take children to such *commercial establishments* as a bank, a large department store to view its inner workings, a greenhouse or florist shop, or perhaps the body shop of an automobile dealer. Finally, field exploration acquaints children with *manufacturing aspects* of the community when children visit a canning factory, a picture and frame store, or a dress-maker's shop. All of these experiences provide important input for the social studies program. The teacher, of course, must carefully structure the experience so it also provides crucial language-learning opportunities.

There are several ways the teacher can provide for language growth in planning such experiences. After introducing the field exploration and explaining it to the children, including some presentation of basic information, the teacher might lead the children to speculate about what they will see, encouraging them to formulate questions to which they want answers as a result of the experience. Some of these may be answered, some may not, but the process of formulating questions, or organizing their thoughts, is a valuable one for children. One group of fourth graders, about to embark on a field exploration to an architect's office, wanted to know the following things:

- Do you [the architect] do all the work yourself? Who helps you and what do they do?
- How do you get to be an architect? Is it hard?
- How do people find out about you? When some-one wants to build a house, how do they decide on which architect to ask?
- After you have made the plans, what happens? Do you go to the place where the house is being built? Can people change their minds while the house is being built?

During a group discussion before the trip, all questions the children wanted to ask were listed on a large chart; various children volunteered to be responsible for finding out the answers. Some answers came up during the course of the presentation the architect made, but others did not, so the volunteers responsible for them asked the questions during the discussion period.

The opportunity to ask questions while on field exploration is crucial to language development and to the writing that will result when children return to the classroom. For this reason it is important that there is a small adult-child ratio while the group is out in the community. This is another way the teacher can structure the experience to ensure language growth. Whenever possible, several adults, both male and female, should be asked to go along on the trip. One purpose is to assure security, but an equally important reason is to provide an adult with whom a child can talk while he or she is on the trip. If the teacher tries to manage a field exploration with only one adult helper, important questions and conversations cannot be raised as they come up. If you are taking a group of thirty children through a factory with only one adult helper, there is a very real chance that some children may not be able to get your attention to ask questions when they occur to them. By the time the group has returned to the classroom, a valid question may well have been forgotten, and an occasion for language use has been missed. It is true that the adult may not have known the specific answer to the question raised, but the adult can enourage question asking and remember questions asked until later. The oral interchange that occurs when children have an opportunity to interact verbally with the adult is beneficial.

Following the field exploration, the teacher should lead a discussion and then ask the children to dictate an account of the experience. By helping them recall what happened sequentially, filling in omitted or inaccurately remembered details, the children can build a coherent, interesting, accurate description of the field exploration. The teacher may help them recall and use the new vocabulary necessary to describe the place visited effectively. The teacher may also encourage children to select from among the many ideas suggested those that are most crucial to a complete account. The dictation, organization, selection, and evaluation of ideas as they are molded into a cohesive account of the field exploration provides valuable language experience. The process is an important base for later objective writing descriptions individual children will do.

WRITING BASED ON OBSERVATIONS: CLASSROOM VISITORS

It is possible, with appropriate safety precautions, to take children almost anywhere in the community for field exploration. Nonetheless, there are times when it is more convenient to bring part of the community, in the form of one or several visitors, to the classroom. Such experiences broaden children's social studies understandings, but they also provide varied language opportunities. Careful planning is necessary to ensure that the possible language benefits actually result from the visit.

As in the case of field exploration, children are introduced to the experience by the teacher. This includes initial familiarization with the vocabulary words related to the visitor, his or her work or interest. If the guest is a weaver, for example, children should be introduced to such terms as *woof* and *warp, shuttle,* and *bobbin* before the visitor arrives. If it is a singer, children need the background of knowing what *diaphragm, vibrato,* and *pitch* mean. If the visitor is a carpenter, knowing what *plane, quartersaw,* and *miter* mean is important. When the teacher talks with the potential visitor to determine the content of the experience, he or she can find out what words it will be helpful for children to know.

Guests who will provide a specific type of language experience for children can also be invited to the classroom. You might invite a parent or other adult who speaks a foreign language. The visitor can demonstrate the language, perhaps telling the children how some common sentences or familiar rhymes are said in the language. Teaching the children to say a greeting in the language, as well as one or two frequently used phrases, is another helpful activity. It is also possible to acquaint children with the concept of dialects by inviting people who have moved to the area from different parts of the country. Children should be encouraged to note how the visitor's speech is like, and unlike, their own. Attention can be directed to phonological (sound) differences, and conversation between the visitor, children, and teacher reveal vocabulary differences as well.

Before any classroom visitor arrives, the teacher should help the children prepare for the visit, encouraging them to formulate a list of questions to which they would like answers. Sometimes these may need clarification. There is an important language lesson that occurs as children grapple with their original question to reshape it so it communicates meaning clearly.

Before the classroom visitor arrives, children may review with their teacher what they have learned about effective listening habits. After the presentation or demonstration, children are encouraged to ask the visitor their questions. Following the visit, children are given the opportunity to write about the experience. This dictated group-story process includes: (a) formulating what the children want to say, (b) organizing the diverse contributions for sequence and coherence, and (c) revising the story when it is completed. Such a total language experience as the one described here builds general language fluency, which will lead to later fluency in individual writing.

WRITING BASED ON EXPERIENCES

Often the teacher will plan an experience for children that is designed to result in writing. One first grade teacher, for example, kept several animals in her room so that children could be involved in caring for and learning about a variety of mammals. During one year, a female cat became pregnant and subsequently delivered several kittens. For the children, watching the experience led naturally into dictating stories about it. The following well-written story was only one of several that children were moved to record:

> This is the mother cat. Her name is Taffey. She is going to have babies. Here, look! A cat is coming. Under the tail it comes. Here it is again, under the tail. Now mother is tired. It is hard to do. So she will rest.
>
> by Stephanie

Many other such "in-class" experiences can be provided for children; writing is a natural outgrowth of most of these.

INDIVIDUAL STORIES

Finding time for group dictation is not as difficult as finding time for individual dictation of stories. The school day is full, and the teacher has many things to do. However, individual dictation is fully as important as are group stories to the development of writing fluency. This is simply because there is, at this stage, such discrepancy between what children can write down for themselves and what they can dictate. Some examples from our first grade children's writing makes the point clear. These samples were gathered in

a lower-middle class school during the fifth month of first
grade. While doing a unit on pets, children were encouraged
both to write and to dictate into a tape recorder. In each
case, both stories were done within one week's time. Todd
was able to write, "My pet is a gray dog and he is a poodle."
In contrast, he was able to dictate:

> My dog's name is Niki and he's seven years old.
> He comes upstairs by me and plays with me. He
> sleeps with me sometimes and I take him for a walk
> in the summer. He's seven years old.

Denise was able to write the following:

> My pet is a turtle. He has a big rock. He has a
> big bowl. He has a nice house. It is a happy home.
> It is a big home.

Later in the week, she dictated this story:

> My pet is a turtle. He has a hard shell. It is green
> and he has a big rock and a big bowl. I love it, and
> he is a nice turtle. Last year we put him in a salad
> bowl and he got out so we didn't have a bowl for
> him yet. He has a big bowl now and it is glass.

Debby's two stories also provide some interesting contrasts. She wrote:

> Do you like your pet? I do. I love my pet. My pet
> is a dog. His friends are very special. He likes to lay
> in the grass.

Her dictated story:

I have a pet with white hair and shaggy furry
hair, and it has black spots. It plays. It's all excited
all the time when I come home from school. It just
loves me and my brother.

Probably the most graphic example of differences between
ability to write and dictate is provided in the two stories
created by Lea. She could only write:

Dog was little love
One box ball
Lea love he do dish [sic]
Love Lea

In contrast, note the fluency with which she dictated the
following story:

My dog is brown. He's got long ears and he's
cute. I love him. I take him for walks sometimes
after school. And when I'm in school, he can't see
me because I'm in class. The teacher saw my dog already. I can pledge allegiance to the flag, but he
can't. He loves me. Sometimes he's good, but sometimes he's not. When he is, I give him chocolate
kisses.

These stories, written by children of average intellectual
and linguistic capabilities, argue convincingly for extended
dictation opportunities. Children at this age do have stories,
and the problem lies in getting them out. Dictation provides
the answer to this problem.

Granted that dictating seems to facilitate language flow,
it is still a time-consuming process for teachers. What can
teachers with twenty to thirty children in their rooms do to
be certain that all children can dictate a story when they

wish? There are several procedures that can ensure that children will feel free to dictate a story when they wish.

- It is wise to set aside a specific time of day and a particular place in the room for story dictation. Children should know, from the time they start school, that there is a time each day when they can go to the story corner if they wish to share a story. The teacher will record what they have to say and then read it back to the children, who can make whatever changes they would like to make. The disadvantage of this approach is that children may have stories they want to record at times when the teacher is otherwise occupied. There are ways to remedy this problem.

- When children are older, but no later than the middle of second grade, simple cassette recorders should be made available so children can tell their story into the machine. There are now machines available that are so simple that it is easy for children to use them. Using such machines makes it possible for children to record stories when ideas come to them and are fresh; waiting until the teacher is available is unnecessary. Stories can be transcribed later by a teacher's aide or other clerical help, so they are available for the teacher to read to the children the next day.

- Though no pressure should be put upon children to develop the mechanical skills of handwriting, the teacher should seize every opportunity to encourage children who are attempting to write. The classroom, of course, contains ample supplies of pencils, ball-point pens, felt-tip pens, crayons, paints, and other writing tools. When a child does write a story and brings it to the teacher, it is important that the teacher accept this offering with interest. It is wise to ask the child who has written a story to read it to you. This provides further encouragement for both writing and reading, and emphasizes the interrelation between the two.

- Utilize older children who have mastered handwriting skills. It is always possible to make arrangements with other teachers in the school for some of their children to come to your room and help record stories. This provides two benefits. Not only will the younger child have more opportunities to record stories, but it will provide practice in writing for older children. This type of practice is particularly rewarding for older children whose mechanical skills are limited. Though they may not be as competent as other children at their own grade level, they will obviously be more competent than younger children. Practice without stigma results, and improvement in the older children's writing is frequently noted by teachers.

- Another possibility too often overlooked is to utilize older people in the community who might be happy to help. Those who are retired are frequently forgotten in our society, yet such people could serve well as scribes for children. Both the children and the adults would profit from such a relationship. Contacting community service organizations could result in a list of names of older people interested in participating in the active life of the schoolroom.

WHAT DOES THE TEACHER RECORD?

In taking down dictated stories, whether group or individual, the teacher is sometimes confronted with the problem of nonstandard usage. For the vast majority of children in schools, this is not a major problem. True, there may be a few such minor slips in usage as the use of *brung* for *bring* or the use of *goed* instead of *went*. These are largely inconsequential. The important point at the earliest stages of dictating stories is to keep the flow of ideas coming. Stories should be written down as they are told to the teacher, who should not interrupt to correct a usage mistake. Many of these minor errors will correct themselves as the child matures and encounters a variety of people who use the correct form.

For groups of children who have a large percentage of usage deviations in their speaking vocabulary, some sort of remedial practice may be needed. This always should be done in periods far separated in time from the dictation periods. When taking dictation, the teacher may well want to note common problems in his or her group. Pattern practice in these usages can be devised and participated in by the group at another time during the day. Because they are held separately from the story dictation period, the children thus do not connect such pattern drill with their own story writing.

The question of the best procedures for teachers to use when working with children who speak a dialect other than standard English has not been answered. The most current idea seems to indicate that children benefit from having a teacher who can understand their dialect; a teacher who is bi-dialectal and can help the children to become so is the ideal.

Such a teacher can, in addition to understanding the dialect, also record it. This would enable the children to dictate in their dialect, rather than trying to tell stories in the school dialect, which may seem very foreign to them.[11] The problem of finding enough teachers who both understand and can write nonstandard English dialects is one which has not yet been resolved.

SENDING STORIES HOME

At the very earliest stages of this writing program, no particular effort should be made to share stories the children have written with the home. If children want to take their dictated stories home, this is acceptable, but it is not encouraged. The two-fold reason for this is simple. *First,* writing is a process that takes a long time to learn. At the beginning of the program we are interested in the process, not the product. The important thing is that children are learning how to compose, and this learning is more significant than what is composed. Many of these early stories will be inconsequential, incomplete, and undistinguished. This is as it should be, for learning to write effectively takes a long time. For instance, one first grade child of average intellectual and linguistic capabilities wrote the following story in mid-January:

> A snow blower. It was whoy [*sic*]. A snowmobile went past.
>
> by Tommy

[11] The strength of writing that results when children compose using their own dialect is amply illustrated in Roger Landrum, *A Day Dream I Had at Night*. Working with children from several minority groups, the author instituted a composition program that resulted in highly original expression by children who previously did not find writing an easy task. The descriptions of how he facilitated the writing should be helpful to all teachers of minority children.

Not a very impressive story, but the perceptive teacher was satisfied with it, realizing that further growth would occur later. Indeed, one month later Tommy was able to write:

> My pet is a big dog. My pet runs fast. Rocke is a yellow dog. Rocke runs away, but we catch him.

The second story represents considerable improvement over the first, yet obviously much remains to be done. The teacher, who sees growth over an extended period of time and in many children, is able to understand the vital importance of these first hesitant compositions.

Second, most adults, including parents, have very conventional attitudes about correctness in writing. These attitudes are deep-rooted and difficult to change. Misspellings, incorrect punctuation, and usage errors, especially on papers sent home, are vulnerable to parents' attitudes about correctness. Yet, at these early stages in the program, the teacher purposely minimizes these problems in favor of giving attention to more crucial matters of organization, clarity of thought, and unity of ideas. For these reasons, it is wiser not to send stories home unless children insist on taking them.

EVALUATION

From the earliest stages of this program, the teacher is concerned with evaluation. Because of the assumptions made in Chapter 1 about writing being a skill, attention must be given to children's accomplishments in becoming better writers. This is in contrast to other approaches, which seem to assume that much of the improvement in writing skills occurs as a result of simple maturation. Here is a typical comment of writers who believe this is so: "From further opportunities to compose . . . and from much exposure . . . to literature, more extended, stronger writing will almost certainly ensue." [12] The question is, does it? Do children develop more effective writing skills from having more opportunities to compose? Perhaps some children do, but it seems evident that these opportunities must be coupled with concomitant opportunities to evaluate their progress in learning to write well. Rather than assuming that children will automatically become better writers, we structure evaluation experiences that help children look critically at writing.

To begin, we evaluate others' writing. The reason for this is simple. Being objective about one's own work, even for adults, is a difficult task. Looking at the words we have put on paper and seeing them clearly is not easy. For this reason, we develop critical abilities in children by asking them to focus on writing by two other groups before turning their attention to their own writing.

First, we focus on the quality of what is included in the reading input component of the program. The teacher who asks children, "What did you like about the story?" is asking for evaluation. Even the very youngest children are willing to tell what they liked about a story you have just read to them. However, it is important, even with the very young, to develop cognitive ability to answer such a question with clarity and precision. Often when asked such a question, children will respond, "It was interesting." The teacher should not be content with such an unfocused response, however, but should pursue a clearer thought by asking questions that will help children focus on *why* they thought a story was interesting:

- What part of the story was interesting?
- What did the author do that made the story interesting?

[12] Alvina T. Burrows, Dianne L. Monson, and Russell G. Stauffer, in *New Horizons in the Language Arts*, p. 192.

- What words in the story were interesting to you?
- Why was the character interesting to you?

These beginning questions are very simple, but as children become more skilled in making evaluations, the questions also become more complex:

- How did the author make you feel sympathetic to the main character?
- How is the speech of the two main characters similar or different?
- How is the description of setting different in this story than in the last one we read?
- Why do you suppose the author made use of a flashback in the middle of the story?

None of these questions is necessary to increase enjoyment of the literature read during the input strand of the program. Children can appreciate what they have heard without ever turning their attention to such questions. The teacher should not ask questions about every piece of literature shared because to do so would likely diminish the enjoyment of literature. However, some of this type of reflection about literature is necessary to develop evaluation abilities in children.

In addition, we can help children evaluate what other children have written. To do this, we may use published literature by children. In the case of books of children's writing, we would use a similar approach to the one described above for literature written by adults. Our goal is to help children become aware of quality in writing and the elements which make for quality.

Another source of stories that may be used to develop evaluation abilities are unpublished stories by children. There are two sources of these. Teachers may share stories with other teachers, exchanging copies of writing by children in other rooms. These writings can be shared anonymously for the specific purpose of evaluation. Another source is stories written by children in previous years. A teacher interested in doing this program with children will keep copies of the stories written by children, saving both good and less effective examples. These also can be shared anonymously to provide material about which children may think critically.

In sharing such examples, a teacher should read both effective and less effective writing. However, he or she would now expand the questions to include some designed to make children think about how a story could be made better.

- Is there anything more you would like to know about the character?
- Is there any place in the story where what the author was trying to say wasn't clear to you?
- Is there any place you can think of a better word than the one the author used? Where?
- Could you have made a more exciting ending for the story? How?

Such discussion helps children see that stories can be improved through rather specific means and that at times they will be asked to evaluate stories, to react to questions with their own ideas. All of this preparatory work leads up to evaluation of their own work. More specific questions useful in evaluation are included in each of the following chapters.

3

CHARACTERIZATION

Who can ever forget the delight of knowing plucky Bilbo,[1] comfort-loving Ratty,[2] adventuresome Miss Hickory,[3] or winsome Princess Lenore? [4] They are memorable, for the authors brought them to life from the printed page. They ceased being simply characters in a story and became, instead, real to us, alive and vital beings about whom we cared. Caring, we remembered them. The ability to characterize, to create with words a description of a person that remains with the reader long after the story is finished, is one mark of a successful writer.

Our focus in this chapter is helping children develop the ability to create characters. To learn to describe the physical and psychological aspects of people (or animals) about whom they are writing is a valuable ability for children. Yet without some conscious help in this area, few children develop naturally the ability to describe a character with economy, effectiveness, and enthusiasm.

[1] J. R. R. Tolkien, *The Hobbit.*
[2] Kenneth Grahame, *The Wind in the Willows.*
[3] Carolyn S. Bailey, *Miss Hickory.*
[4] James Thurber, *Many Moons.*

Often characterization in children's stories is rather flat, presented in general terms or types, as for instance occurs purposely in old folktales. Such limited characterization is acceptable in folktales, where the plot receives major emphasis. Similarly, in children's first writing, description of characters is often limited. We do not want children's ability to characterize to stop here, however. What we are after in this strand of the writing program is a fuller, richer characterization in which the child uses physical and psychological descriptors to build a unified, memorable entity. To accomplish this we must plan a sequence of experiences with characterization. As with the other parts of this approach to writing, the experiences are threefold:

- extensive exposure to literature that presents a variety of characterizations
- writing experiences based on observations the children make of aspects of character
- writing experiences growing out of specific pieces of literature used for motivation.

READING TO PROVIDE INPUT

In planning experiences with characterization, the teacher chooses books to read that present a wide variety of characters: male and female, young and old, rich and poor, real and imaginary. The books chosen are read to children and savored. Sometimes the selections are discussed; at other times they are not. The reading occurs each day; the teacher is aware that children may be assimilating unconsciously some of the aspects of successful characterizations exemplified in what they are hearing.

Young children should encounter books presenting vital images of both male and female characters. Many authors

have written stories that contain convincing presentations of boys as main characters. You might try:

Rufus M by Eleanor Estes.
Young children will enjoy the adventures of indomitable Rufus, whose determination often gets him into trouble. First graders will remember with empathy their feelings about learning to read as Rufus learns to write his name so he can get a library card. This is a thoroughly delightful book, which speaks directly to children today, despite its age.

Massacre Inlet by Edward S. Fox.
Older children will enjoy the story of Guy, one of a shipload of French Huguenots shipwrecked on the Florida coast during a hurricane in 1565. The special relationship between Guy and his father is warmly and convincingly drawn. Characterization differences between the French, the hostile Spanish, and the Indians make for compelling reading.

Stories with girls as the main characters should also be shared in the reading program. You might try:

Tell Me a Mitzi by Lore Segal.
Martha wants a story, so her mother makes one up about Mitzi, a self-possessed little girl, capable of all sorts of things her parents don't suspect. Another story recounts the complex problems of having colds; a third shows Mitzi's brother Jacob as very strong minded. The consciously ugly children mark the illustrations as the distinctive work of Harriet Pincus.

From Lupita's Hill by Bettie Forsman.
Older children will find the story of interest. Lupita, a poor Mexican girl, has predawn visions of a beautiful white dress. She, her friend Christina, and the gringa girl, Amy, are all convincingly drawn. The contrasting characters are well developed.

It is important that children encounter books that present convincing portrayals of people of all ages—young people, old people, and the interrelations that develop between them. For example:

Did You Carry the Flag Today, Charley? by Rebecca Caudill.
Share this beautifully realistic story with children in order to appreciate the successful way the author has developed the main character, a young child. Caudill evokes the first grade child convincingly, not by telling what he is like, but by showing us through his actions. The authenticity of Charley's speech adds to the characterization.

Mr. Angelo by Marjory Schwalje.
This is a whimsical story of a little old man, a gifted cook but a poor business manager. The characterization is developed by overstatement, which doesn't diminish its effectiveness. Mr. Angelo is believable because of the consistency with which he is portrayed. Abner Graboff's bold, colorful illustrations advance the story line.

Two books that present well-developed characterizations of *both* young and old, and that explore the interrelations between them are:

Longbeard the Wizard by Sid Fleischman.

For younger children, this charming brief tale contrasts greedy King Barbos the Old, who was rich and wanted to be richer, with King Sander the Young, who was poor. Barbos' greed is contrasted beautifully with the simple, ingenious character of Sander whose magic and quick wit eventually save him.

A Likely Place by Paula Fox.

Children who are Lewis's age, ten, will sympathize with his considering running away. Harassed by teachers, parents, indeed even by his classmates, Lewis is ineptness personified. When his parents go on a trip, an eccentric babysitter lets Lewis meet Mr. Madruga. Despite the disparity in their ages, they become fast friends. In solving his friend's problem, Lewis discovers that he is not as inept as he thought.

Characterization examples should also include stories about both rich and poor. Two books which explore the lives of rich children are:

Eloise by Kay Thompson.

Though the book about Eloise's adventures is very familiar to adults who were growing up when it was published, children today may not know Eloise. They would certainly be delighted to encounter her as she careens madly through the expensive elegance of the Plaza hotel, as depicted raffishly in the illustrations by Hilary Knight.

Linnets and Valerians by Elizabeth Goudge.
> Robert, Betsy, Nan, and their dog Absolom are un-
> happy about being left with their autocratic grand-
> mother by their father who has gone off to Egypt.
> Though financially comfortable, the children are re-
> stricted at every turn by the grandmother, who has
> very definite ideas. How they escape her domination
> forms the basis for a series of adventures.

Books describing the lives of poor children include:

Blue Willow by Doris Gates.
> A Newbery Award runner-up, this sensitive story of
> Janey Larkin's shifting world as the daughter of
> migrant workers is appealing to intermediate grade
> children. It skillfully draws a convincing picture of
> the precarious existence of an affectionate family de-
> pendent upon the crops for their livelihood.

Gertrude's Pocket by Miska Miles.
> Living in a dying coal town in the Cumberlands,
> the Tollivers eke out an existence severely limited
> in economic ways, but rich with a strong sense of
> family pride. When a wealthy couple lose their
> way and get help from Gertrude, she receives a
> windfall in the form of a dollar of her very own.

Children should also experience characters in both real
and imaginary stories. A very *realistic* presentation of both
plot and characters is included in:

"Hey, What's Wrong With This One?" by
Maia Wojciechowska.
> Three young boys drive their widowed father to
> distraction with insistent pleading for a new mother.

Each imagines a different kind of mother and plans a way to get her, since their father doesn't seem to be doing anything about the problem. A wealth of small detail creates a beautifully drawn, realistic picture of the children and their father.

The Traitors by James Forman.
Intermediate grade children will enjoy the story of Paul, Kurt, and Astrid, Germans caught up in the Second World War. The change in characterization, as the young people respond to the pressures of war, provides ample material for discussion.

Imaginary stories for children are also useful for considering character development:

Stuck with Luck by Elizabeth Johnson.
Young children can profitably think about the characterizations in this fantasy, the story of Tom, whose problems only begin when he discovers a leprechaun. He learns the complex problems caused by the leprechaun's tendency to grant his every (including inadvertent) wish.

Enchantress from the Stars by Sylvia L. Engdahl.
The story takes place in a locale not fixed in either time or space. The adventures of Georyn, youngest son of a poor woodcutter, are of interest to older children. The book includes many characterizations worth study.

The first responsibility of the teacher in developing ideas about characterization is to select books representing such a variety of character types. Those listed above are only samples; from the wealth of books available, teachers will have no trouble finding examples of the categories listed and of other categories to share with children.

In addition to a wise selection of books that present a variety of characters, the teacher has another responsibility. This is to help children think about *how* the author develops the character.

PHYSICAL CHARACTERIZATION

Frequently we learn about a character through the physical description the author gives us. For example, in *A Girl Called Al* we get a strong impression about Al as we learn what she looks like.

> Al is a little on the fat side, which is why I didn't like her right at first. . . . She walks stiff like a German soldier, and she has pigtails. She is the only girl in the whole entire school, practically, with pigtails. They would make her stand out even if nothing else did. . . . Al's pigtails look like they are starched. She does not smile a lot and she wears glasses. Her teeth are very nice, though, and she does not wear braces. . . . Al is a very interesting person.[5]

Another vivid physical characterization is one by Judy Blume in which the author tells about Margaret's growing up.

> When she smiles like that she shows all her top teeth. They aren't her real teeth. It's what grandmother calls a bridge. She can take out a whole section of four top teeth when she wants to. She used to entertain me by doing that when I was little.

[5] Constance C. Greene, *A Girl Called Al*, pp. 10–11.

. . . When she smiles without her teeth in place
she looks like a witch. But with them in her mouth
she's very pretty.[6]

A similarly effective description is included of Laura, the
biggest girl in the schoolroom.

The teacher wasn't in the room when we got there.
. . . There was this girl, who I thought was the
teacher, but she turned out to be a kid in our class.
She was very tall (that's why I thought she was the
teacher) with eyes shaped like a cat's. You could see
the outline of her bra through her blouse, and you
could also tell from the front that it wasn't the
smallest size. She sat down alone and didn't talk to
anyone.[7]

In another example James Flora [8] describes character by
indicating physical appearance in an unusual way. In this
case he describes an invisible animal. Leopold himself can't
be seen, but his footprints can be if you look carefully. You
can also tell he has "such big toes, and long fur" when he
walks across your hand. Minerva, the little girl he adopts,
knows where he is by seeing the crumbs resting on his invisible whiskers. She can further tell where he's going by the
trail of inedibles (e.g., candy wrappers) that he leaves behind.
It's a delightful example of physical characterization and
could easily form the basis for a writing lesson with children.
You might, for instance, have children make up another invisible animal, or perhaps human, character. Children could
explore in writing the advantages and disadvantages of being
invisible.

[6] Judy Blume, *Are You There, God? It's Me, Margaret,* pp. 18, 25–26.
[7] Ibid.
[8] James Flora, *Leopold, the see-through crumbpicker.*

FULLER CHARACTERIZATION

We are not content with simple physical characterization, however, as we want children to explore more involved dimensions of personality. It is crucial to consider such questions as:

- What is the character like "inside"?
- How does he/she feel about things that happen in the story?
- How does he/she react to people, ideas, and events?

For this reason, we share with children examples of fuller characterization. Discussion may be necessary to point out what the author is doing. For instance, we can use the description of Al's mother.[9] Near the end of the story, the girls go to Al's apartment to find help because something is wrong with their friend, Mr. Richards. The description of Al's mother at this point is only physical.

> When we got to Al's apartment her mother was still in bed. She had on an old bathrobe that looked sort of like the one my mother wears, and she did not have all that stuff on her face. She looked very pale, and her nose looked as though she had been blowing it a lot.

The girls ask for her help in finding out what is wrong with Mr. Richards. Here Ms. Greene gives us further insight into what Al's mother is like inside. "She got up and said, 'I'll have to change. I can't go down like this.' " Though she is willing to help, her appearance is a pervading concern. The children finally convince her to go the way she is be-

[9] Greene, *A Girl Called Al*, pp. 115–16.

cause of the urgency of the situation. Despite her acquies-
cence, Al's mother is still concerned about her appearance.

> Then we went down on the elevator and Al's mother
> still had her bathrobe on, so it was lucky we didn't
> have to stop until we got to the basement. She had
> a big wad of tissues in her hand. She said, "I do
> hope it is nothing serious," and "I look such a
> fright, I hope we don't run into anyone."

It's this kind of internal characterization we are interested
in helping children develop. The examples analyzed above
are simply samples of the type of character development and
interaction available in books for children. As teachers acquaint themselves with children's literature, they will find
many other stories equally useful in developing understanding about internal characterization.

We should not only help children think about characterization, but also about how the different characters in the
story interact. This can be begun with stories for the very
young:

Sam by Ann Herbert Scott.
> Sam tries to interact with his mother, brother
> George, sister Marcia, and his father, all of whom
> are too preoccupied with their own concerns. When
> Sam uses the young child's usual approach to solv-
> ing such problems, his family finally responds. The
> characters are all skillfully drawn by the author and
> in subtle monochromatic illustrations by Symeon
> Shimin.

A book for older children can also be used as a basis for
discussing the ways characters react to each other:

Getting Something on Maggie Marmelstein by
Marjorie W. Sharmat.
Hilarious treatment of the conflict between Maggie
and Thad is largely due to the realism of the characterizations. The dialogue is convincingly childlike,
and the descriptions of the school and the teacher
are uncanny in accuracy. The class play sequence is
reminiscent of the play in *Harriet, The Spy*.

LANGUAGE AND CHARACTERIZATION

In many instances character is enhanced or further deline-
ated by the language the characters speak. To help children
think about the ways dialogue brings characters to life, you
might acquaint them with the work of Lenski. *Strawberry
Girl*,[10] for example, uses the dialect of the Florida crackers.
Marguerite De Angeli also has written many books useful
for studying the ways language further defines characterization. *Thee, Hannah* makes the point quite effectively.[11]

In addition to these, there are books available in which
the language of the characters changes. One example is
found in a book about Abraham Lincoln, whose life changed
as he grew older.[12] The author gives us many samples of the
dialect Abe spoke as a child:

"One-two-three—I drapped one, Pappy."
"Kaint we go now?"

[10] Lois Lenski, *Strawberry Girl*. You might also try *Cotton in My Sack*,
which is set in Arkansas, or *Judy's Journey*, about the life of migrant workers
in the southeastern part of the United States.

[11] Marguerite de Angeli, *Thee, Hannah*. Others in this series of books
using Pennsylvania Dutch dialect include *Henner's Lydia* and *Yonie Wondernose*. In *Petite Suzanne* the author has created an approximation of French
pronunciation of English. In *Jared's Island* the dialect is integral to the
story of a young boy and his brother who are lost at sea. In *The Door in the
Wall* the dialect of English spoken in London permeates the book.

[12] Clara Ingram Judson, *Abraham Lincoln*, pp. 12, 23, 31, 180, 196. The
same stylistic device is used by Genevieve Foster in *Abraham Lincoln*.

"No, Mammy," Abe replied, "jest sayin' the lesson."
"Kin we start tomorry?"

This contrasts with the polished, slightly formal dialect he spoke toward the end of his life.

"Are you not overcautious when you assume that you cannot do what the enemy is constantly doing?"
"If I know my heart . . . my gratitude is free from any taint of personal triumph."

This is adult language, of course, different than the shorter sentences of a child spoken earlier in the book. It is also, however, a very polished style of speech, learned by Lincoln who knew that the dialect spoken in his home was not appropriate in the different world into which he had moved.

Language difference due to situation is beautifully developed in an exciting adventure tale set in rural England during the Second World War.[13] Early in the story the children talk among themselves very naturally, using short, direct sentences. For example, the first time Lucy returns from Narnia, this conversation ensues:

"But I've been away for hours and hours," said Lucy.
"Batty!" said Edmund, tapping his head. "Quite batty."
"What do you mean, Lu?" asked Peter.
"What I said," answered Lucy. "It was just after breakfast when I went into the wardrobe, and I've been away for hours and hours, and had tea, and all sorts of things have happened."

In contrast, toward the end of the story, after Aslan has installed them as Queens and Kings of Narnia, their con-

[13] C. S. Lewis, *The Lion, the Witch and the Wardrobe*, pp. 18–19, 150–51.

versation is quite different. Following the White Stag into the forest, they pause to consider following it further, especially since they have seen a strange tree which seems to be of iron. Edmund says:

> "Fair Consorts, let us now alight from our horses
> and follow this beast into the thicket; for in all my
> days I never hunted a nobler quarry."

They wonder at the wisdom of this, and comment on the "tree," which is revealed to be a lamp post. King Peter remarks:

> "Marry, a strange device, to set a lantern here where
> the trees cluster so thick about it and so high about
> it that if it were lit it should give light to no man."

In the Narnia adventure language varies because of situation. Several authors have explored this idea. In *Me and Arch and the Pest,* John Durham gives us a sensitive portrayal of the differences between classroom speech and oral language.[14]

Following the reading of such a book, in which language differences are apparent, it would be a beneficial challenge to ask intermediate grade children to write a story of their own in which the character's language changes to fit the situation.

POINT OF VIEW

Another aspect of characterization is point of view, a concept to which older children should be exposed. Much literature is written in third person, in which a narrator tells what is happening to the characters in the story. A different approach is first-person writing, in which the author speaks as

[14] John Durham, *Me and Arch and the Pest.*

if he or she were the character in the story; this allows much freedom as well as providing some restraints. Intermediate grade children should be exposed to both types of narration so that they will begin to see the range of possibilities each provides and also the inherent disadvantages in each.

Often the stories you share with children will be told in third person, that is, narrated by the writer. Third person is an economical way of conveying to the reader much information that simply could not be conveyed had first-person narration been used. An example of this approach is found in:

Horrible Hepzibah by Edna M. Preston.
> The story is told about baby Hepzibah and how she dominates everyone she encounters, including her parents, her neighbors, and even an ugly beast. Everyone, that is, until her aunt for whom she is named comes to visit. Then the story takes a surprising turn.

A follow-up activity to any story told in third person is to ask the children to imagine themselves as one of the characters and to rewrite part or all of the story from that character's point of view. Writing as if they were Hepzibah, her mother or father, her aunt, or even Vanilla, the little girl next door, can result in some interesting writing by the children. In doing such a writing task, they learn about first-person narration.

One teacher of first graders tried this technique. After reading a version of "Cinderella" to her children, she allowed those children who were interested to retell the story as though they were one of the characters.

> I am Cinderella, dressed in rags. I live with my stepmother and stepsisters. I sleep on ashes by the

fireplace. I have to clean the house every day.

The Prince was giving a ball. My mother wouldn't let me go to the ball. Then I had an idea. I asked my hazel tree. Of course it was magic, and so was the mourning dove.

First I had to curl up my hair in a bun. Then I asked for a pretty dress and some slippers. Then I was almost ready for the ball.

I danced with a handsome prince. He said he wouldn't let anyone else dance with me, so I danced with him until the clock struck midnight. Then I had to go, but I said to myself, "I'll see that prince again," and I did see him again.

One night I lost my slipper, and the prince found it. He searched and searched, and finally he came to the last house. He tried the slipper on both step-sisters, but it didn't fit. Finally he came to *me*. That slipper was mine, and then it happened. I was his bride. I lived with him in the castle, and the dove, and we lived happily ever after.

by Karen

My mother died. I was living alone with my father. Then one day my father decided to get married again. That is when all the trouble started. My step-mother was mean.

One day an invitation came from the castle. It was a ball in honor of the Prince's birthday. I couldn't go. But I had a magic hazel tree with a fairy dove in it. I made my wish for a beautiful colored gown, and a crown with diamonds, and a pair of golden slippers.

But my dove gave me a warning, "You must be home before midnight." I got home before mid-night, but I lost one of my slippers. When the

Prince finally found me, he took me on his horse to his castle to be his bride.

by Julie

A teacher of third grade children tried the same technique in using "Snow White and the Seven Dwarfs." Her children wrote the following stories, assuming the role of one of the characters:

The Evil Queen

When my mirror said I wasn't the fairest of them all, I jumped up and down squawking my head off. I ordered the Huntsman killed, and tried to kill Snowdrop, but those dwarfs saved her. When I finally killed her for good, I was jumping with joy.

After a while I went to my mirror to make sure I was the fairest of them all. When I found out that I wasn't, I growled so hard the castle shook. When I was put into those iron shoes I yelled and jumped until I died.

by Steve

The Good Queen

One day I was sewing at the window, and I pricked my finger. It dripped three drops of blood. The snow was white, but then it was red. I was thinking of having a girl with black hair, rosy cheeks, and white skin. Then I did have a baby, and the baby had black hair, rosy cheeks and white skin. I love my baby. I think she's the loveliest girl in the world.

But now I am very sick. I think I'm going to die. I hope my baby is going to have a nice life.

by Charlotte

The Huntsman

I went to the forest, and Snowdrop was running about twelve feet ahead of me. We were entering the woods, and I took my knife in a hard grasp. Snowdrop was by a tree, and I threw my knife. I missed. I just couldn't do it. I told her to go off into the forest. She went. A fawn leaped into my path. This time I took my sword and stabbed the fawn. It was bloody murder. I brought back the lung and liver. The queen ordered me to take it to the cook to be pickled. I was glad that bloody mess was over.

by Jeff

These stories illustrate one of the strengths of first-person narration: it is more direct, because it is the character him-/herself talking. More information of a personal nature can be presented in shorter compass than if such information had to be described. The disadvantage is that nothing can be included that wouldn't *logically* have been thought or spoken by the person telling the story.

We get helpful insights into what Ox is like, both physically and psychologically, in his opening, first-person description.

I'm big for my age. And fat, too. I mean really big. I'm not as fat as I am big, but I'm fat enough. I guess it's puppy fat, because my grandfather—the one who made the money—was about six feet eight, and he was fat when he was young, too.[15]

The story of an unhappy boy in a plush Palm Beach

[15] John Ney, *Ox*, p. 5. In contrast, you might want to share Ethelyn M. Parkinson, *Never Go Anywhere with Digby*. A delightful story narrated by Joel, a preteen-age boy in the homespun tradition of **Homer Price**, who has an eccentric friend, Digby, able to empathize with ants.

setting is far removed from most children's experience, but since it is treated realistically, children can respond to Ox's problems.

The effectiveness of first-person narration is also shown in the following section from a book narrated by a rather unusual girl.

> I was the only girl I ever knew who could hang by her toes from the exercise bar in our upstairs front sun porch. It was about my only accomplishment. And I always realized it wasn't important. It wasn't like being able to ripple "Barcarolle" over the piano. . . . There was no real future in toe-hanging. Unless, of course, you planned to make a career of testing crash helmets.[16]

These input sessions should occur regularly, during which time literature is shared, enjoyed, and sometimes, though not always, discussed. Other sessions also should be planned in which children are asked to observe people (potential characters) and then write about their observations.

OBSERVATION LEADS TO WRITING

Observing people in their environments gives children a base upon which to build written descriptions. Close observation of other children forms a way to begin developing characterization ability. Simple physical descriptions can be managed by children as young as kindergarten age.

We might, for example, ask for two volunteers to come and stand in front of the group. Children are then asked to notice what they can tell orally about the children. The teacher should encourage the children to tell whatever they

[16] Christie Harris, *Confessions of a Toe-Hanger*.

notice, accepting all comments but minimizing whatever negative ones might be given.

Such an observation and discussion session serves two purposes. First, it helps develop observation skills as children look at the "subjects" minutely for some descriptor they can name. Second, it develops oral fluency as children are encouraged to put their observations into sentence form.

This initial discussion provides an introduction to description skills. After the discussion session, the teacher should provide time for those children who want to dictate a brief description of one of the children in the room.

The purpose in using two subjects is so children can begin simple comparing. Teachers may encourage the use of comparison words: *higher* or *taller than, bigger than, redder than, longer than,* and others. Using pairs of subjects also provides the encouragement that may be necessary for children of this age.

Later, after this process has been tried several times, the teacher should help children reflect upon the types of observations they have made, drawing out categories of descriptors. These can be put on a chart and kept in the room for further reference as children progress through the sequence of characterization sessions.

The teacher wants children to eventually notice that a good physical description of a person often includes such aspects as height, weight, hair (style and color), clothes (style and color), and posture.

After they have developed ideas about description, the teacher may want to have children try the more difficult task of attempting a description of themselves. The children should be given an opportunity to observe themselves in a full-length mirror, which may not be possible at home. They should be encouraged to notice all the different types of physical descriptors that previous oral discussions revealed to be important. The children may refer to the chart developed earlier to see that they have observed all the important points. Then, individual children are encouraged to dictate or write a description of themselves. Because of the preliminary observation and discussion of physical features, such dictating or writing should present no problems but should be seen as an easy extension of the earlier group activities. Young children recently dictated or wrote the following descriptions:

I have long, curly eyelashes. I'm wearing a Winnie the Pooh shirt. I have dark brown hair. I have pretty pants on. I'm a happy boy and a nice boy.

by Brian

I have a loose tooth. My size is in-between. I'm a nice girl. I'm pretty each day. Sometimes I wear a ribbon, and sometimes I have a pony tail.

by Mary

My eyes are greenish blue. My eyebrows are brown. My eyelashes are black. I have lots of freckles. I have short, light brown hair. I am not too skinny, and not too fat. My legs are not too long, and not too short. I have a middle-sized nose. My teeth are white. My head is round.

by Karen

I have long legs like my Uncle Ted. He used to be in the Army. Now we don't know where he is. I miss him. I also have powerful legs, like my Uncle Ted. I have two big teeth, and they are good for digging into apples. My eyes are as sharp as eagle's eyes. I am a tall boy, and I'm rough and tough, and I can help people when they're hurt.

by Brian

I am not skin and bones, and I am not fat. I have hay brown hair. My eyes are blue. My skin is rough. I am four feet, three inches tall. I have four-inch fingers, and two-inch toes.

by Jeff

I have short, blond hair. I like long hair. My eyes are green. I am kind of peach, or tan. I have a big nose. I have long toe nails. I wear big shoes because I have big feet. My birthmark is on my ear. I am a little over four feet. I weigh 70 pounds. I have big muscles. I have rough skin.

by Paul

OBSERVING WITH OLDER CHILDREN

Observation with older children is handled in a slightly different way. The teacher may ask children to select a "secret friend," whom they observe during an entire school day. By observing throughout a day, children can notice such things as modes of speech and movement in addition to the factors listed above. Children are encouraged to jot notes to help them remember what they have observed. Toward the end of the day, children are asked to discuss the kinds of things they observed, and following discussion they are given time to write a description of their secret friend. Intermediate grade children wrote the following character descriptions after such a day of observation.

I've known him for a long time. Ever since I came to this school he has been my friend. Maybe not so secret, but he is with this assignment. He has a sensible personality. He's kind, and sometimes forgets things. He's not so good in running, yet he makes up the work in art. He wears glasses and has long eyelashes, brown hair, and smooth skin. He is very funny sometimes.

by Andrew

He sits about fifteen feet away from me. He sits near Mark, and close to the wall. He is a hall monitor. He also likes to help Miss _____. Today he is wearing a blue shirt. He has white hair, and blue eyes. He is about two inches smaller than me. He has a soft voice at times. Sometimes he laughs at people. He is very nice. The teacher says that he is doing very good work.

by Tony

This person is very polite, nice, and funny. He likes rocking on a chair, and always looks at the clock. When the person agrees, he nods his head. The person can make very funny expressions, and sometimes squints his eyes.

He is pretty tall, wears "cool" shoes, and pretty clothes. He has a cute walk—not too long, not too short. The person likes to suck on the ends of pens, and he feels his hair and itches his head. The person uses the hands for expression. This person is always busy. He talks pretty loud.

by Katy

The person I am writing about has short, string hair. It is dishwater blonde, with bangs. It always looks uncombed.

The person has certain habits. I have noticed that he always pounds his hands together when he is looking at someone else. He is always arguing with people, and saying, "I didn't do anything."

He never has a pencil, so he is always asking for one. He usually is talking when an assignment is given, so he usually doesn't finish it, and doesn't know it. He talks a lot anyway.

He is wearing a short sleeve shirt that looks too small. The shirt is bue, and his pants are partly red. The shirt looks really old. He has an interest in shot guns, and sky rockets.

by Ginny

An alternate way to sharpen observation skills and develop understanding of how to write characterizations is to introduce an observation game. All the children put their heads down on their desks so they cannot see. The teacher walks through the room and taps two children on the shoulder, choosing children who look somewhat alike, are about the same size, height, coloring, and have other similar features. These two walk to the front of the room and stand side by side, facing away from the group. The remainder of the children then guess who each subject is. Choosing children of similar appearance encourages closer observation than the previous assignment in which just one child was the subject.

Such observing assignments are important because:

- We all tend to overlook those things with which we are familiar, including the people we see each day. This conscious focusing on people and attendant writing experiences emphasizes the importance of observing skills.
- They provide a base for a discussion of the importance of observing skills to an author. Characters in books are memorable because of the accumulation of detail; they seem real to us because of what we know about them. True,

descriptions frequently are made up, are of imaginary people. But the details are often drawn from skillful observations the author made of real people and then incorporated into his descriptions. This is the point of which children are too often unaware.

The third component of this program, writing experiences directly related to, or based on, pieces of literature, is crucial to the success of the program. Some sample experiences are described below.

CHARACTERIZATION BASED ON LITERATURE

As early as kindergarten, children can be helped to think about characterization as presented in literature. In addition to simply thinking about how authors create characters, children should also be given opportunities to write characterizations based on literature.

For example, five-year-olds enjoy Giant John,[17] and one of the follow-up activities after sharing this book could deal with characterization. After reading the book, we might ask children what John was like. We know what he was like physically and can make a list of these characteristics. But we also know what he was like "inside," that is, we know what his personality was like. Discussion with young children often reveals that they know John was:

- Fun loving (shown in his fondness for dancing)
- Thoughtful (in his consideration for his mother)
- Obedient (in wearing his rubbers when told to)
- Willing to work (as he helped at the castle)
- Responsible (when he helped repair the damage he did).

[17] Arnold Lobel, Giant John.

Discussing these characteristics with children helps them see that an author tells us not only about physical aspects of character but also helps us understand personality. A writing assignment based on this story could ask children to describe a friend for Giant John. Prewriting discussion should focus on the sorts of people John might like. Then children could do a character description. At the earliest stages of writing—perhaps in kindergarten when children will dictate their ideas—a simple description is enough. Older children may want to weave their descriptions into an adventure for John and his new friend, thus giving attention to simple plot development.

Following the reading of the book, several writing possibilities exist. One child wrote a description of what she thought Giant John was like:

> Giant John is tall and he has shaggy hair. John has a funny round nose. He wore a green shirt. John wore rubbers. He has an umbrella. He is a hard worker. He was very poor. If he had a friend, he would be tall and playful. They would fly kites made out of thousands of trees. His name would be Jack.
>
> by Sarah

Some other children wrote their thoughts about what it might be like to be a giant:

> If I were a giant, I would eat ten watermelons, five cantaloup, and 100 pumpkin seeds. I would ask someone to make clothes for me. I would sleep outside. I would make people laugh. I would make the ground shake. Trees would fall into the river.
>
> by Julie

If I were a giant, I would bring trees to my mother. I would sleep outside of a house. To eat, I would have 51 potatos. I would not be scared of a fox. I would look out of a big magnifying glass to see the newspaper. It might be good to be a giant. It might be bad to be a giant.

by Stephanie

If I were a giant, I wouldn't be a bad giant. I would play outside because I would be too tall. If I broke things I would fix them up again. I would snore. My sister, the giant, would sleep outside too. We would play together. We would sing together. We would have fun.

by Margo

In another classroom, children were asked to write about what they thought it would be like to meet Giant John.

I would like to have Giant John be my friend. I could go to a picnic on his lap. In summer, if I got too hot, he could blow a breeze. We could go water skiing. But if we went skiing, if John fell down, the boat might tip over. In autumn, he could rake up all the leaves and bury me in the leaves. In winter I could use him for a sled.

by Tracy

Once upon a time there was a giant, and his name was Giant John. One day I met him. We were going to my aunt's lake. I didn't want to go in the water, because it was cold. He helped me get in the water. He took me across the lake. We went fishing. He got all the fish.

by Elizabeth

A group of first grade children was asked to describe a friend for Giant John.

> Giant John would have a big friend. They would barbecue a cow and a pig. They would drink a whole lake of soda, and have an ice cream mountain for dessert.
>
> by Kenny

> Giant John would pick a little friend. The giant would tell what it's like to be big, and the little one would tell what it's like to be little. They would play and go swimming.
>
> by Daphne

> Giant John would have a giant friend. They would get a rope and a board and make a swing. They would take down a tree, and hang the swing from the tree like a mobile.
>
> by Stephen

Two third grade children also described a friend for Giant John.

> Once when John was walking in the woods, he heard a voice: "Hi, there." He looked around. "I'm the Big California Redwood. I'll be your friend." "O.K.," said John. They played together. They played chess and checkers and Monopoly and other things.
>
> Then one day a lumberjack came and was about to cut the redwood down, but John said, "Don't you dare cut him down. I'll get all the trees you want, but please don't cut down my friend!" "Your friend? Ha, ha. What a friend. I've seen better friends. What can it do?"

"Well, it can talk, and play games," said John.
"O.K., talk."
"My name is Reddy."
"I don't believe it. Let's see it play."
"O.K."
"Play chess." Reddy played chess, and the lumber-jack let him go.

by Erika

Giant Jim
He is 100 feet tall. He has a deep, low voice. He is very nice and helpful. He lives in a cave in the Rockies. He is forty-nine years old. He likes to work for other people. Whenever a tornado comes, he grabs it and makes it into a cloud. Whenever there is a flood, he fills his water pitcher. And that's Giant Jim.

by Jeff

Another story which can be treated in the same way features a lonely little old man marooned on an island.[18] If you use the story with primary children, following the procedures described above, a useful writing assignment can result. Children enjoy creating a friend who could come to live with the little old man, and in the process of such creation they learn more about characterization.

After hearing the story, two kindergarten children dictated the following descriptions of a friend for the old man.

A sister could clean the house. She could help him fish. She could play games with him. She could help row the boat. She could cook his fish.

by Scott

[18] Natalie Norton, *The Little Old Man.*

A little old lady would make him breakfast and bring him aspirins if he's sick. She'd give him orange juice if he's sick too.

by Beth

A second grade child wrote the following:

Once there was a little old man. He was a nice little man. This man had a garden. He liked to go fishing, and he liked to rest. One day he was resting, and he saw a boat, and somebody was in it. It was a boy, and his name was Jeff. Jeff was lucky to find land, because he was out in the water for a month. When the man heard that, he let Jeff live with him.

by Pat

Third grade children responded to the story with the following compositions:

The Old Man Got a Friend

One day the little old man saw a big ship. The ship blew in on shore. Then he went into the ship. He looked all over. Then he saw a person tied up. It was a man who was his age, 60 years old. Then the little man untied the other man.

"Boy," said the man, "that is not comfortable being tied up."

This man was a cook. By this time the little old man was really hungry, so the cook cooked him a big, big supper.

Then they went to catch some fish. So they went out, and caught so many fish that they lasted so long the old man thought he would have fish coming out of his ears.

by Monica

The Man and the Little Old Lady

One day the little man decided to go find a friend to go fishing with him. So he went into town. Then he found a friend. Her name is Natalie. She has lots of fish mounted on plaques. He asked if Natalie liked fishing, and she said, "I love it." So they went fishing.

One day the little lady said, "Should we get a house by the river?" "O.K.," said the man.

Then they went fishing again, and they caught 2,000 fish. But they had a problem, because the next day was Thanksgiving. No one eats fish on Thanksgiving.

But the lady said, "Well, we don't have to have both," and the man said, "O.K.," and that's the end.

by Natalie

CHARACTERIZATION IN LITERATURE FOR OLDER CHILDREN

A favorite story of many children, *Charlie and the Chocolate Factory*,[19] provides a good experience with characterization. Following the reading of the book, discuss with children both what is known about the characters and what can be inferred about them. Dahl offers a rich characterization, not only including simple physical features, but also more complex psychological factors. Discussion of the characters can be done in references to the list of character descriptors prepared earlier in the sequence of writing sessions. After analysis of what Dahl has done in his story, children are asked to write another character to add to the story. If there were six tickets to Mr. Wonka's factory instead of five, who might the other child be? What would

[19] Roald Dahl, *Charlie and the Chocolate Factory*.

this child be like, physically and psychologically? Children who had experienced this motivation wrote the following stories:

> The name of the person is Wormy Glob, and he loves to lick stamps. He says that his tongue feels lonely if he doesn't do that. He is always sticky and dirty, because he gets his hands sticky and wipes them on his clothes. He can lick stamps fast because he has two heads, and two of everything else.
>
> by Scott

> The next winner is Sliver Dollerr. He is a very interested coin collector. When he heard that the ticket was made of gold, he thought he might try to get it.
>
> Sliver always wears green and white. His hair is very short, so he can see coins more clearly. He is very skinny, because he's too busy on his coins to eat. He's a bore if you aren't interested in coins, because that's what he's constantly talking about.
>
> by Ben

> The name of the character is Sam Seavert. He is tall, and thin, and his face is long and sad. He has brown eyes, long hair, a tiny nose, a big mouth, and he's a baseball fan. Most of the time he wears a baseball uniform, with metal spiked shoes. He even sleeps in it. He goes to every Mets game. His hobbies are baseball, and tobacco chewing. He is repulsive, and a poor loser. Also, he's not friendly, except to his team members. He always carries his glove and ball with him.
>
> by Roger

An alternative story equally well suited to such treatment is *The Long Secret*.[20] The author has created a bizarre set

[20] Louise Fitzhugh, *The Long Secret*.

of characters; Zeeny (Beth Ellen's mother), Norman, and the other Jenkinses are unusual to say the least. Children enjoy the story because of the characters; writing a description of another child or adult to be included in the plot is an interesting challenge.

OTHER LITERATURE-BASED WRITING POSSIBILITIES

Many works of literature can be used to help children grow in understanding characterization and how to create it. Three additional examples are included here to illustrate other possibilities. As with all strands of the program, the teacher should feel free to search out other literature that will be of particular interest to his children.

Some stories present well-defined characters who remain essentially the same throughout the story. The appealing characters in stories by Milne are examples of this type of characterization.[21] Type or stock characters like this, who react in predictable ways, give a sense of continuity to stories. In introducing this idea, try the chapter suggested below. Read the episode to children and have them discuss such questions as:

- How did Eeyore feel at the end of the story?
- What clues does the writer give us to help us know how he felt?
- How did Eeyore's sadness help make his birthday happier?

The main problem in the episode—someone's birthday being forgotten—is an effective stimulus to writing. To begin, you might have the children enact their responses to the question: What would you do if it was your birthday and no one knew? Dramatizing responses to such questions

[21] A. A. Milne, "In Which Eeyore Has a Birthday and Gets Two Presents," in *Winnie the Pooh*, pp. 72–89.

as these is frequently a helpful way to motivate children to write their responses.[22] After children have dramatized what they would do, encourage them to write a response to the question.

In other books the main character changes. Children should also encounter such stories for the stimulus they provide to think about how a character changes. *Crowboy,* a book about the changes that occur in a small boy, an outcast in his school, provides ample opportunity to study characterization.[23] The story is told in third person; we learn much about Chibi through the narrator's eyes. You might read the story through page seventeen. At this point, lead a discussion about how the children feel about Chibi. Make a chart listing all the words or phrases that describe Chibi. Then finish the story. Discuss with children how their perception of Chibi changed by the end of the story. It would be helpful to have them think about how Mr. Isobe affected what they think of Chibi.

Another book, *The Selfish Giant,* in which character change is apparent can be presented in book format, though it is also available in filmstrip format.[24] The change in heart that occurs in the selfish giant when he is able to respond to the children is good stimulus for discussion of reasons why characters change. In using the story with children you might encourage them to consider such questions as:

- Why was the giant called selfish?
- Have you ever known someone who was selfish? How did he or she act?
- Have you ever felt like keeping something to yourself?

[22] Further information on how story dramatization can lead to writing is included in John Warren Stewig, *Spontaneous Drama.*

[23] Taro Yashima, *Crowboy.*

[24] Oscar Wilde, *The Selfish Giant.* Also available as filmstrip with accompanying record from Weston Woods (SF 132).

- If so, how did your friends act when you did?
- What happened in the story that helped the giant change?
- Do we usually need a reason before we can change?

This story is particularly effective to use with children in motivating them to write a story in which a character changes. Before writing, have the children consider ways in which people could change. Make a list of ways the children think of that people change. Such a list might include:

sad to happy	frightened to confident
angry to content	gullible to wary
stupid to smart	foolish to prudent

After such a motivating discussion, have the children choose one of the ways that were identified and create a person who changed in this way. The story can describe what made the character the way he/she was at the beginning, and the way the change occurred.

EVALUATION

As in all the strands of the writing program, evaluation is taken to mean a process done jointly by child (author) and teacher. The principles underlying this procedure were explained on pages 58–59, so a few specific suggestions about how to help children evaluate characterization should suffice here.

As in other evaluation, the teacher approaches the problem of helping children consider their work through the questions asked. For example, after reading one of the children's stories to the group, the teacher might ask such questions as:

- Why did you like the character in the story? What things made him or her interesting to you?
- Were there other things about the character that you wanted to know? What were they?

Later, children might be asked to consider such questions as:

- What details about the character did the author share with us that made him or her seem real? (Or imaginary, if that is the case)?
- Did the character act the way you thought he or she would? Why or why not? If not, how did you think the character would have acted in the situation?
- Did the way the character interacted with the other characters seem believable to you? Why or why not?

Some evaluation may be done in group situations, with the teacher always being careful to do two things:

- Preserve the anonymity of the author. There is no need to tell who wrote the story unless a child wants to acknowledge authorship. What is to be focused on is the story itself.
- Emphasize the need to evaluate positively. Even when a child is asked how he or she might have developed the character differently, the emphasis is on how it might be done *differently*, not better.

Evaluation is also done individually as the teacher meets with a child to discuss more fully his or her growing writing ability. Sometimes these conferences focus on the story just written; at other times a longer view is taken of the stories included in a writing file. To help evaluate growth in writing skill, it is useful to have a file of compositions written previously by the child. A manila file folder can be used to save each child's writing so that evaluation may take place at the end of every quarter, semester, or some other convenient time. Such an arrangement takes up little space in the classroom, little time to set up and maintain, yet results in immeasurable benefits in evaluation conferences. Because the teacher is interested in assessing growth in writing skills, which develop slowly, it is necessary to have previous writing as a reference in noting progress.

In having a conference with a child, the teacher might help the child explore such questions as:

- Do my stories show that I am learning to write about a variety of people? Can I tell effectively about old and young people, men and women?
- Are my people becoming more believable? Do they say and do things that *might* happen within the confines of my story as I've written it? (This question is designed to help children think about character in relation to the types of stories they write. What is appropriate character behavior in a fantasy is quite different than appropriate character behavior in a true tale.)
- Am I improving my ability to make people more real? Do the many physical, psychological, and language details I include seem to make the people alive rather than flat, like silhouettes?
- Do I try to personify something? Can I convincingly make something inanimate come to life?

4

AN EXCITING
PLACE TO BE

Have you ever tramped through the woods on Haw Bank,
searching for hazel nuts and blackberries with Keith and
David? [1] Or have you ever been jostled around in the dark-
ness of Gideon's pocket? [2] Or stood over the wood stove
helping Ma make curds? [3] Or walked the strip of rubber
matting up to the librarian's desk with Rufus? [4] If you've
delighted in any of these experiences, you'll never forget
the specific sense of place the author created. Each of these
environments is so distinct, so unlike any other place you've
experienced, that the memory of the place lingers long after
the book has been read.

One of the writing tasks we set for children is description
of environment, for in most successful writing, the writer
gives us a clear and vibrant understanding of where the
action takes place.

To help children learn to write descriptions of setting

[1] William Mayne, *Earthfasts*.
[2] Rumer Godden, *Impunity Jane*.
[3] Laura Ingalls Wilder, *Little House in the Big Woods*.
[4] Eleanor Estes, *Rufus M*.

effectively, we use the same approach as in other strands of the program. That is, we plan three types of experiences:

- extensive exposure to literature, which the teacher reads orally to the children
- writing experiences related to observations made by the children
- writing experiences based on literature

To provide the first type of experience, the teacher reads many stories depicting different types of settings and talks with children about how the writer created a sense of place. In choosing, the teacher carefully selects literature that evokes setting through a variety of means.

Some settings give us memorable *visual* images. Sometimes these are scattered throughout a book as in the case of *Gone Away Lake*. Enright gives us vivid images to help the reader understand the several locations she describes. Among these she writes about the outside of an old house: "on one of the square porch pillars a crop of fungus stuck out like turkey feathers." [5] Other writers, in contrast, give the reader a complete picture of setting before beginning the action. Because the apartment in which the boy and his grandfather live is crucial to the action, the author of the story "Wild Bird" describes it for us fully before the story begins.[6]

Some writers give us clear and distinct sound images. Sometimes, especially in books for young children, sound images are conveyed through repeated refrains. In *The Enormous Sweater* the somewhat eccentric little old lady's incessant knitting is accompanied by the "click, clickity,

[5] Elizabeth Enright, *Gone Away Lake*, p. 37.
[6] "Wild Bird" is one of three stories included in Florence Parry Heide, *The Key*. Strong, unusual stories that might be called gothic, these are not for everyone. Nonetheless, they are memorable and striking because of their themes and the author's sensitive style.

click" of her needles, and the "creak, creakity, creak" of her rocking chair.[7] The use of these sound words serves two purposes. They help children see how a strong rhythm can be set up to enhance the story line, and they are also used to describe elements in the setting.

In *Behind the Magic Line*, a book appealing to intermediate grade children, we get a clear impression of a setting established primarily through sound images. In this section the little girl, Dozie, listens to the night.

> She knew it was late at night. She knew that before she opened her eyes. The sounds at night were very different. The streetcars didn't run very often, and there were no voices outside. Right here, in the heart of this great gray city, with the whole dark blowing night outside, it was quiet. If you listened . . . you could hear a far-away rumbling . . . not heard unless you really listened for it, that was the city traffic . . . the continuous beat of a city that never slept. But here in the big square room it was so still that she could hear her brothers and sisters breathing and could tell one from another.[8]

Another effective set of sound images helps establish the setting in *Nobody's Cat*, a story for intermediate grade children about a scruffy alley cat, wise in the ways of his world. "In the nights, he heard the thud of heavy feet hurrying along the sidewalk, the whine of tires in the street, doors slamming in the alley." Late one afternoon, as the cat walked along, he heard sounds as "music rocked from a high window." Further on "there was no sound." Instead, there was a cat with a saucer of milk. During the resulting fight,

---

[7] Adelaide Hall, *The Enormous Sweater*. The wonderfully wacky illustrations in collage by Abner Graboff considerably enhance the total effect of the book.

[8] Betty K. Irwin, *Behind the Magic Line*.

"they sprang . . . screaming and biting, thumping and tumbling." The alley cat escaped. "When the alley was quiet, he lciked his leg where it was matted with blood." [9] The book is particularly effective, as can be seen above, in the alternating of sound and silence. Each alternation helps establish a different part of the setting.

Less often do authors give readers *spatial* or *tactile* images. These need to be pointed out to children. For spatial images, read either *The Mousewife* or *Mouse House*.[10] Designed for younger children, both of these contain fine descriptions of space. In the first the author has created an effective contrast between the cozy space behind the fire fender and the dangerous open spaces of the rooms themselves. Another contrast is drawn between the constricted space of the gilt cage in which the dove is imprisoned and the open field in which he used to fly. In the second book the author has contrasted the pleasant, tiny spaces of the doll house with the overcrowded lack of space in the flowerpot which serves as home for the cellar mice.

Tactile sensations describing the setting of the story are included effectively by Craig in writing about little Jeremy, who "felt the cool morning air move across his cheek." After this he picked up the peach, which "was warmer than the morning; the sun had already touched it." Then he held it, "warm against his curved palm and fingers." He walked along, "smoothing the roundness of his peach with his fingers." He lay in the grass "for a long time, and the sun warm and then hot on his bare legs, the peach warm and round in his hand." [11]

Olfactory aspects of settings are less usual than other descriptors. Enright does utilize this device effectively in telling us that "The breath of the house came out to them.

9 Miska Miles, *Nobody's Cat*, pp. 3, 6, 8.
10 Rumer Godden, *The Mousewife* and *Mouse House*.
11 M. Jean Craig, *What Did You Dream?*

It smelled old." [12] A more extended olfactory image is included in the setting by Snyder. She writes about a boy, Dion, whose explorations of a posh downtown department store had been a hobby since he was eight years old.

> After the ordinary winter world outside, a dirty
> gray with a cold, wet wind, inside . . . [the store]
> was like being on a different planet. The warmth
> was clean and smooth and loaded with something
> that was too high class to be called a smell. . . .
> I was still standing inside the door trying to sort
> out the smell—I'd gotten about as far as new cloth
> and leather and perfume and dollar bills.[13]

Of course, most setting descriptions are done using a combination of sensory images. Sight and sound images are included by Estes for instance. She establishes a very clear sense of place when she describes where the forlorn little girl, Wanda, sits in the classroom.

> She sat in the corner of the room where the rough
> boys who did not make good marks on their report
> cards sat; the corner of the room where there was
> the most scuffling of feet, the most roars of laughter
> when anything funny was said, and the most mud
> and dirt on the floor.[14]

In a less usual example, *Walter, the Lazy Mouse,* the author describes setting, not by telling us what *is* there, but by telling us what is no longer there! Young children

[12] Enright, *Gone Away Lake.* This is also available in excerpted form in Edna Johnson et al., *Anthology of Children's Literature.* A very complete reference including works from ancient myths and legends to modern fantasy and fiction, this is a helpful book for a teacher interested in implementing this program.

[13] Snyder, Zilpha Keatley. *Eyes in the Fishbowl.*

[14] Eleanor Estes, *The Hundred Dresses,* pp. 3–4.

especially enjoy the predicament of Walter, who is so slow
that one day his family forgets about him and moves away.
Coming home (hours late) he opened the door to the
kitchen:

> He saw that the kitchen looked very strange. There
> was no stove, no table, no chairs. He went to the
> pantry and it was bare; not a crumb of food could
> he find. Walter went into the dining room; that too
> was empty. He went into the living room; not a
> bit of furniture was in it. Walter ran upstairs and
> into his room. His bed was gone, his chair was gone,
> everything was gone! He looked into his closet and
> even his clothes were gone! [15]

Some descriptions, like those used as examples above, may
tend to present setting simply in its physical aspects, detail-
ing only the tangible elements of the environment. With
other writing, we get both objective description of the setting and some indication of the character's reaction to it.

John Donovan's novel for late intermediate grade children
provides such an example. The description of his mother's
apartment when Davy moves in is clear contrast with his
former environment. The author includes both physical description and also some of Davy's reactions to his new home.

> Mother's house is in the middle of the block. It was
> built in 1834 and has high ceilings. There are a
> couple of fireplaces in her apartment, and a nutty-
> looking porch over the kitchen of the people who
> live under her on the second floor. We're all shiver-
> ing with the cold when we come in, and it's the
> back porch Mother wants to show us first. She calls
> it her terrace, and I can see right away that she

---

[15] Majorie Flack, *Walter, the Lazy Mouse.*

> thinks Fred can live out there. I tell her that Fred
> loves heat, and if she will show me where I'll live,
> I'm sure Fred can squeeze in there too.

Davy's evaluation is implied by the author in the description of his bedroom:

> It's all boy, all right. She has had it paneled and
> has had some skinny drawers built in a skinny
> double-decker bed. She's got a strange collection of
> stuff on the walls, and she tells me they are from
> Childcraft. They're great, of course, but they're for
> kids about five. . . . The mattress on my bed is OK,
> and it's pretty neat that Mother had another bed
> built on top of mine. Both of them are so narrow
> though that I'm not sure I'd want to sleep in the
> top bunk. That will be for people I invite, I guess.[16]

The above are simply examples, chosen to show the range of setting descriptions that abound in children's literature. The teacher, reading widely, will find many other equally good examples to share with children. In reading to children, we should pause to discuss these images after we have enjoyed them for their aesthetic quality. We should let children react to them, responding in their own words to the unmistakable sense of place the author has created.

SETTING IN CHILDREN'S WRITING

The second type of experience we provide for children in this program is writing based on observation. This is necessary because often setting is described minimally, or not at all, in children's writing. The experiences we plan will help children develop their skills of describing setting.

[16] John Donovan, *I'll Get There. It Better Be Worth the Trip*, pp. 34–36.

Initially, we might have children write about their class-room. As in the case with characterization, we begin by heightening children's awareness of what is around them. With young children, have them close their eyes and listen to the many sounds they can hear. This is a valuable listening lesson to aid general language arts development, but in addition it serves as a helpful base for writing.[17] Have children make a list of sounds they hear. Later search for descriptive words. The children may have heard a bell. What descriptive words can they use to tell about it? Was it shrill, sharp, tinkling, loud, high, or what? Encourage fluency with descriptive words by accepting all the words children contribute at this early stage in the sequence.

Let children describe their visual sensations: deal with colors, shapes, and sizes of things in the room. With young children simple enumeration is enough: see how many names of things can be included. With older children, work for answers to more sophisticated questions:

- How many triangular (or other geometric) shapes can you see in the room? [18]
- Find all the reds in the room. Can you put into words how they are different? (This is raising sensitivity to subtle distinctions. Red is not magenta, is not cerise, is not vermillion, is not fuchsia, etc. Try this activity using any color that is available in a variety of shades or hues. On a day when several children are wearing blue, for example, have the children observe carefully the

[17] For a description of how such an experience develops listening acuity, and specific suggestions for planning listening activities leading to writing, see John Warren Stewig, *Exploring Language with Children.*

[18] Helen Borten, *Do You See What I See?* An older book, this is still available for heightening awareness to environmental components. Through sensitive words and well-designed visuals, the author helps children see the multitude of shapes around them.

differences and put into words what they take in
through their sense of sight.)

- How is the space in our room different than the
space in the hallways or in the office?

Tactile sensations need to be explored. Children should
be encouraged to explore the surfaces in their classroom
with their hands. Provide a sensory input by letting children touch a variety of contrasting surfaces. Then realize
the vocabulary output by challenging them to put into words
what the surface felt like. How is the surface of the desk
different than the surface of the floor? How is the surface
of the wall different than the surface of the blackboard?
Many such opportunities to compare and contrast results
in heightened sensory awareness and increased ability to put
into words the sense input.

Later, have children work in pairs, with one child blindfolded and the other child acting as leader. The leader's
job is to provide different sorts of tactile experiences by the
way he or she leads the blindfolded child around the room.
Then roles are reversed. At the conclusion of this exploring
experience, children are again encouraged to discuss their
sensations, to put into words or phrases what they experienced through their senses.

Following a variety of such experiences, children are encouraged to write either a group description or, with older
children, individual descriptions of their classroom.

After such a motivation, a first grade child wrote this
description of her classroom:

I like our room, because it is nice.
Our room has pets and stories.
It has lots of our writing, and things we made.
We have three pumpkins.

There are lots of kids in my class.
I will tell you about our pets.
We have five gerbils and one lizard.

by Heather

Third grade children composed the following descriptions
of their rooms:

The counter in our room is smooth.
The paper feels soft and smooth.
The dictionary feels smooth.
The volcano feels rough. It smells like vinegar.
The carpet in our room is rough.
When people walk it makes a tip-tap kind of sound.

by Sherri

My classroom is on the side of the school. It is
noisy because it is on the side. We hear the blowers,
kids outside, cars and sirens and squeaky chalk.
We touch smooth things like our desks, tables,
books and chairs. I sit in the back now. I see kids
walking past the door and down the hall. We have
a looking center and a reading center and a research
center.

by Lynn

I have a noisy classroom. The desks are facing
south and east. Some of the desks are facing south-
east. Our desks are smooth on top and smooth in
the pencil tray. The chalkboard smells good, but
it tastes bad.
The paper is usually bluish-green.
We can hear sirens and kids.
We have two colorful, smooth globes. One is big,
and the other one is smaller.

by Steve

My classroom has pink walls, and lots of books. The windows look like squares. The blower covers are smooth one way, and rough the other way.

The chalk dust smeels, and just plain dust smells.

I can hear the trees blowing, the lockers slamming, voices in the hall, kids outside and cars on the street.

by Monica

With older children, we might not restrict the observation to the classroom, but in addition, explore the area around the school. Again, use the blindfold approach to emphasize sound and touch.

When intermediate grade teachers planned such an experience for their children, the following stories were written.

When I was walking down the hall I felt the wall, and it was hard. Then I felt the floor. It was smooth and hard. Then I went outside and felt the side of the door. It was bumpy. I felt the fence. It was jagged and sharp. Then I felt a rock which was prickly and bumpy.

Then I heard something. Someone was scratching the walls. I heard people singing and walking down the hall.

Then I went outside again, and heard people talking, and felt something jagged and tough. I smelled something, which was like burning, and I tasted something sour.

by Dawn

I felt very scared. It was a very new feeling. Touching, feeling, hearing, but not seeing. When I was blindfolded, suddenly all of my other senses took over. I didn't know where I was, but I had some ideas. Everything was new to me. Things feel different when you have all your senses and when you don't.

by Greg

I felt alone and scared.
Mysterious, slanted tree.
Round, wet, and cold pole.
Happy shouts, laughing.
Bumping into hard things.
Falling into a big hole.
Stumbling around.
Rough, hard surface.
Crumbly dirt.
Soft and slimy grass.
Floating, lightly mist.
Strange dips.
Unidentifiable space—
Weird happenings.

by Conley

I was walking on hard, rugged asphalt. Then I started going down a hall, and I was back on the same rugged asphalt. I started walking, and I ran into a fence. I spun around and staggered. Then I moved my feet to see what type of land I was on. It was rocky like gravel, but you could slide on it. A person spun me around and I ran into a plant. I smelt it, but it smelt like a dry plant. I tasted it. It tasted like a smooth, sour leaf. I could hear the leaves rustling, the rocks rumbling, but I did not know where I was.

by Peter

I was in a very sunny spot. I heard talking, the loud rumbling of vehicles, and crickets strumming their legs. I tasted a thin substance, and I liked it. It tasted sweet, like the first cherry ripe on a cherry tree. Some things were rubbing against my leg. I picked up a dry, crumbly object that was thin. I raised my hands before me and felt a cold, prickly, round object. I walked ahead about three steps and felt a metallic, round object with sharp things at the top. Do you know the mysterious place? How would you describe it?

by Katy

Dear Mom,

Today for our writing assignment we went on a journey—sort of. One person was blindfolded and their partner led them around until they didn't know where they were. Then they stopped the person, and the blindfolded person had to smell the area, feel the area, listen to the area, and taste the area. Then they had to try and figure out where they were.

Geni went first, and she found out where she was after a short while. When my turn came Geni led me around and I was so scared. Finally she stopped and I just could not figure out where I was. After that we had to write about our experience. That is why I am writing this letter to you.

Some of the things I heard were kids laughing and a noisy furnace near the eighth grade wing. I felt the hot sun burning on my back, and a rough piece of wood. I smelled the wetness of the leaves on the grass. I tasted the sour and bitter taste of the grass.

Love,
Karen

LITERATURE EXPERIENCES

The third type of experience we provide is a writing problem based directly on a piece of literature. In this case the teacher chooses some literature by an adult author that will serve as motivation for a writing session.

We might use the barn description from a perennial favorite, *Charlotte's Web*.[19] Reading this to children we would point out that it is a description of Charlotte's home, the barn. Then we would shift to a consideration of the children's own homes. Discussion of the sights, smells, sounds, touches, and tastes of their homes encourages children to share what they remember of their sense impressions of their home. The observation assignment is to experience their home—or perhaps just a room in their home—that evening. The following morning they are given an opportunity to write their sensory impressions in a description of their home in the way that White has described Charlotte's home. Intermediate grade children wrote the following stories after such a literature-based motivation. Some of the descriptions were very simple, dealing briefly with one room of the house.

> As I walked into my bedroom last night I heard a slight squeak in the floor. I saw my red, white, and blue wallpaper. As I am walking on my carpeting bare footed, it feels soft and warm. It smells like something burning. It is probably the fireplace.
>
> by Mitch

> When you come into our kitchen, you will probably hear the whistling of the boiling water, the crackling sound of the ice machine, or even my

19 E. B. White, *Charlotte's Web*, p. 13.

father loudly tapping on the table impatiently waiting to be served. You might see my mother taking the glasses out of the dishwasher, or my dad helping make Jello.

Sometimes at dinnertime you can smell the very juicy steak sizzling, or even smell the soup.

Maybe my mother will let you taste some yummy pizza, or a lovely chicken. You can feel the large table and chairs, and even the hard candy in the center of the table.

by Kevin

Dear Aunt Ruth,

One day I came home and nobody was here. There was a note on the table. I picked it up from the table, and it said, "I'll be home soon. There is a chicken in the oven." I went over to the stove and smelled the chicken. It smelled very good. Then I went over to the window and touched the smooth glass. It was wet and slippery, since it was cold outside. Then a big truck went by, and it made a lot of noise. After a while I was thirsty, and I got a drink of water. I went to the cupboard right above my television set, where there were dishes and cups. I took the cup which had a rough side. I turned on the hot water by accident, so I ended up drinking hot water!

Love,
Debbie

One sixth grade writer described her adventure in an unfamiliar house.

A Mystery in a New House
I walked into the house. The carpeting was rough and bumpy. I lay down on a soft, soft sofa. I got

up and went to get the newspaper. I smelled the
fresh air. I came back in, and listened to the soft
music on the radio. The lady called me to dinner.
I felt the flatness of the table. I picked up the silver-
ware and it felt cold and hard.

When I first tasted the meal, it was delicious. The
potatoes tasted hot with pepper. The meat was
salted just right. The squash was stringy, but still
tasted good.

After dinner I saw the man and son fighting for
fun or play that looked very funny. They also made
very loud noises. I got up and walked around. I
saw the lady cooling dessert. I also saw the two
little girls playing together.

Now I have to go to bed, so good-night, or good-
bye.

by Brenda

Sense of smell is important in this description, which
incorporates many sensory descriptors and leads to an unusual last paragraph.

My house excites your senses quite a lot. It smells
like wind—open and free. It also smells like sand
and the seashore, because it's made of sandstone.
It gives you a sort of hollow and empty feeling, because it's so huge, but it also gives you a feeling of
warmth and contentment.

If I were to walk around our whole house feeling
with my hands, I'd feel the roughness of the sandstone and the smoothness of the wood. Both of
these substances totally cover our house. If I feel
carefully, I'd feel the warm, cozy feeling of shag
carpeting. Sometimes I might be able to feel the
sheer, cold clearness of glass and windows. I could

smell the sandy smell of our house, and feel as if I were at the seashore.

Another of my favorite places to put my senses to work is my bedroom. There I can best taste the sand in my mouth from the stone. I can smell what's brewing down in the kitchen perfectly from here and it always makes me hungry. My room smells of fresh clean-cut wood and animals.

As I sit here writing I wonder as I hear the crickets chirping from my window, and my kitten gently purring in my lap if there possibly could be a sixth sense?

by Molly

Another vivid setting description is included in *The Borrowers*.[20] Early in the book, the author includes a description of the little people's home; the living room and Arriety's bedroom are particularly clearly drawn. Try reading the section to children and discussing their reaction to it. Then ask children to observe their own rooms at home that night. An early morning writing period the following day resulted in these stories when teachers tried this idea with children.

My bedroom is clean.

It is colorful because the bed has a flowered quilt, the chair has circles in the covering and the floor is a solid yellow. The soft yellow goes all around the room from end to end.

My animals feel very soft and cuddly.

I feel good about my room because it's nice to play and work and sleep there.

by Anne

Third grade children wrote the following descriptions:

20 Mary Norton, *The Borrowers*.

My living room is an olive kind of color. We have a soft shag rug that's an olive color, too. The pillows on our couch have lots of color, and we have a soft bench of the same material. We have a piano that my grandfather got for a wedding present. The lamps are all glass, except for the shades, that feel very rough and prickly. Our living room looks big, but it's not.

by Sheri

My living room sounds pretty in the summer, because you can hear the birds sing. My living room looks empty, because it is big and we don't have much furniture. My favorite chair is a very colorful one. It can spin around. It is my favorite room in the whole house.

by Nancy

In my bedroom, it's all sports. There are a lot of pennants in my room. On my bed and pillowcase there are all the football teams you want to know. My mom and dad bought me a desk attached to a cabinet. I have the cabinet behind. It is a closet with two doors. Its color is green. One side is paneled. And there are posters on it.

by Jeff

Another possibility with younger children is *Mouskin's Golden House*.[21] One kindergarten teacher used this for a session on descriptive writing. After listening to the story and discussing it, two of her children dictated the following descriptions of rooms in their homes:

Our kitchen has a counter and shelves. The sink has water that always drips when we turn it off.

[21] Edna Miller, *Mouskin's Golden House*.

Sometimes my mom puts more antiques on the window. The table sometimes has stuff from our breakfast on it.

by Beth

The bed is soft. It has a railing. Those are the things that keep me in. Daddy and Mommy don't want me to fall out. I lie on the bed. I have a pillow on it. The bed spread has pretty colors on it.

by Kathryn

A first grade child, after hearing the same story, dictated the following description:

My bedroom is a room a boy would like. It has soldier curtains with cannons on them at the windows. My bedspread is like a car. It has everything a car has—a steering wheel in the middle, brakes at the bottom, wheels on the side. It also has an emergency brake and mirrors on the side. It has doors and lights, license plates and a trunk.

by Daniel

OTHER LITERATURE-BASED WRITING POSSIBILITIES

The possibilities for developing ideas about setting are virtually limitless. Teachers interested in developing this writing competency may use whatever stories they find to augment the suggestions included here. One further suggestion is offered to illustrate the approach we have described—a picture book showing how it can be used with very young children.[22] Use the story on a day when foggy weather has

[22] Alvin Tresselt, *Hide and Seek Fog*.

softened and obscured the elements in the landscape. The actual fog and the story will heighten children's awareness of their senses of hearing, touch, and smell. Take the children outside to experience the fog and its effect. Explain to them that this is their time to play with the fog, to take pictures of it in their mind, smell it, hear it, taste it, and touch it. After a sufficient time, meet with the children in a group inside and have them share their impressions. Make a chart of descriptive words, phrases, and images. Follow this up by having each child draw, perhaps with chalk, their impressions of the story and the actual fog. Then let children dictate their experience into a tape recorder. When finished, play all the stories for the children, letting each hold up his or her picture to share as the story is playing.

Such an experience as this can lead easily into further weather writing problems, designed to help children perceive how weather colors and changes our environment and our behavior. Another aspect—the effect of time of day on an environment—can also be explored. Descriptive writing about the playground at nine in the morning, at noon, and at three in the afternoon could point up differences that occur as the day progresses. These can be contrasted with a writing problem that asks them to compare, for example, 9:00 A.M. in the winter and 9:00 A.M. in late spring in geographical areas where the changes are marked.

EVALUATION OF SETTING

As with other elements in this program, we want children to develop the ability to look at their own writing and evaluate its effectiveness.

In thinking about setting with children, we begin very simply. We might use some of the following questions in a group discussion after children's stories have been read:

- Can we tell where the story took place?
- How did the author tell us about the location?
- What words did the author use that were particularly helpful in letting us know about the place?
- Are there other things we would like to know about the setting? What are they?

Teachers should use such questions as they sense are appropriate to the maturity level of the children and to the particular story or stories being shared. It is not intended that you use all the questions every time you share children's writing with the class. It is possible, of course, to use such questions—appropriately reworded—to help a child during an individual conference evaluate his or her own work.

With older children the questions should become more sophisticated. For example, in having a conference with an intermediate grade child, your purpose might be to have the student review and reflect upon several stories written earlier. In this context, using stories from the writing file, it might be helpful to explore such questions as:

- Am I getting better in my ability to look at an object and write a clear, concise description of it that will let my reader understand what I saw?
- Am I getting better at combining descriptions of several objects into a paragraph so that the objects seem to fit together logically?
- When I write made-up descriptions, are they clear and convincing so that my reader can really "see" the location?
- Am I getting better at being able to eliminate parts of my setting description that are not necessary?

5

DEVELOPMENT
OF IDEAS
ABOUT PLOT

It is necessary to develop some rudimentary ideas about plot with children, simply because interesting characters and an evocative setting are of little final effect unless something exciting happens in the story.

Children are fond of action in stories, so it is easy to interest them in plot problems. The writing problems included in this chapter are designed to give children conscious insights into ways plot may be manipulated by writers.

PARALLEL PLOT CONSTRUCTION

A simple and effective way to begin developing an understanding of plot with young children is to introduce the idea of parallel plot construction. This idea was described in chapter two, page 40, but will be further developed here.

To do this, the kindergarten teacher shares a folktale with the class. After the telling or reading of the tale, the teacher leads a discussion, the purpose of which is to help children recall on a basic cognitive level what happened in the story. Plot summarization is a skill children will find useful later in reading programs, and developing the skill in this way also helps them understand that plot is an element of story construction that can be thought about. After a review of the plot, children are encouraged to dictate their own version of the story.

We are here asking children to do what another writer [1] also suggests when she recommends we ask, "Can you construct a story in which the plot follows the same path as the one which we heard?" Evertts comments on such parallel construction, using Alice Dalgliesh's story for older children, *The Bears on Hemlock Mountain.*[2]

In an initial experience of this type, we might ask the question and encourage children to write whatever they can, related to the story that has been read. As soon as children are ready, we structure the situation more carefully, suggesting that they could:

- Rename the characters.
- Change the number or type of characters. For example, in the Pancake versions described on pages 38–40 you will notice that in some stories the Pancake encounters only people. In other versions he encounters both animals and people.
- Change the nature of the characters. In some cases, for example "The Pancake," a completely different main character might be created. In

[1] Eldonna Evertts, "Dinosaurs, Witches, and Anti-Aircraft: Primary Composition," in *Language and the Language Arts,* ed. Johanna S. DeStefano and Sharon E. Fox, pp. 387–395.

[2] Alice Dalgliesh, *The Bears on Hemlock Mountain.* The story, a miniature "tall tale," is an adaptation and expansion of an old Pennsylvania tale. As in other old tales, the plot involves a main character, sent from home to perform a task, who needs and receives the help of a stronger person to accomplish the task. Children will enjoy the rhythmic repetition of the refrain.

other stories changing the nature of one character is interesting. Help children consider such questions as, "What might have happened differently in the story if one of Cinderella's sisters had been kind to her?"

- Change the events or the sequence in which they happen. Help children consider such questions as, "How would the story have been different if each of the three pigs had built a house of brick?" Or, "How might the story have been different if all three had lived together?"

Second grade children who had listened to their teacher read "The Pancake" wrote the following stories. Some of them follow quite closely the pattern established in the original story, others show more variation. In all three there is rich detail and commendable attempts at writing conversation.

> Once there was an old lady and she had two watermelons. She said, "I might as well eat them." "Oh, no, you aren't eating us! Come on, let's go." "Hey, come back here," said the lady. The watermelons met a cow. "Don't go so fast," said the cow. "I want to eat you up. MMMMMM, that one was good. Now where is that other one?" Then the watermelon met a hen. "Stop, I want to play with you." "O.K. let's go." "Wait, I can't swim." "Hop on my back," said the hen. Whoops, that was the end of the other watermelon.
>
> by Patrick

> Once there was a peach that was growing on a tree. One day a man came along and said, "I want that peach." When the peach heard that, he got

down and ran as fast as he could. Soon he met a man, and the man said, "Stop, stop!" But the peach rolled along. Soon it met a boy. The boy said, "Stop, stop!" But the peach rolled along. Soon it met a girl. The girl said, "Stop, stop!" But the peach rolled on and on. Soon it came to a pig. The pig said, "I'll get you away from them." So they ran away into the woods. Soon they came to a stream. The pig said, "I'll take you across. Hop on my nose." All of a sudden the peach was done. He had been eaten.

by Jenny

Once upon a time I bought a pack of football cards. The gum jumped out. I started to chase the gum. I ran out the door. I slipped on the edge of the door. He got away. He ran to a hen. The hen said, "Stop, I want to eat you." So the hen chased the gum. Then he ran to a cat. The cat said, "Stop, I want to eat you." "I didn't stop for the hen, and I won't stop for you." Then he ran to a cow. The cow said, "Stop, I want to eat you." The gum said, "Well, I didn't stop for the hen, and I won't stop for you." So the cow started to chase the gum. He ran to a dog. The dog said, "Stop, I want to eat you." The gum said, "Well, I didn't stop for the hen and the cow, so I won't stop for you." Then he ran to a farm. The farmer was feeding the horses outside. He ran to catch the gum. The horses ran away. The man said, "Stop. I won't eat you." The gum slipped, and the farmer caught him. He shared the gum with the others.

by Greg

A third grade child wrote the following version, in which the personified food didn't need to run away.

Once there was a poor old lady. She said to herself, "Why shouldn't I have a little snack of or-
anges?" So she took out an orange. All of a sudden
the orange said, "Why don't you eat another orange? How would you like to be eaten?" and with
that the orange bit her nose, and that was that!
From then on the lady knew better than to eat a
smart orange.

by Nancy

Still later we might help children analyze the basic plot
structure of the story to see how many stories use the same
structure. Evertts points out that the Dalgliesh plot involves
a very simple set of events; such a plot structure can be the
basis for a variety of writing problems.

Children probably stay strictly with parallel plot construction very briefly. Before long they are experimenting, building upon the basic plot line that has been presented. But
they should be helped to see that there is nothing wrong in
borrowing a kernel idea, or plot structure, from a story they
have already heard. Rather, they should be encouraged to
take an idea and make it uniquely their own. Great composers have for hundreds of years borrowed themes and
motifs from earlier composers. The same is true of writers
and of painters. A fascinating aspect of art history is to trace
the adaptation of a composition idea by many different
painters. Often such an idea, or theme, can be traced
through several hundred years. If such is the case with
mature, producing professionals in the arts, and if such a
technique facilitates the writing process, why should we be
afraid to let children build on a plot they have already
heard? [3]

Many folktales are, in plot, quite simple. Children enjoy

[3] Another statement of the values of parallel plot construction is included
in A. B. Clegg, *The Excitement of Writing*, p. 19.

hearing them read or told. Such tales provide helpful material for young children to use in developing their skill of parallel plot construction.

PLOT COMPLETION EXPERIENCES

Many teachers have made use of the idea of plot completion, that is, reading a story to children and stopping before the end so children are motivated to finish the story. The technique works with children at all age levels.

Almost any story can be read to a crucial point in the action and then stopped so children can finish the action in their own way. Old familiar folktales, as well as more recently available ones, can be used in this way.

One teacher used "Little Red Riding Hood" [4] with her third grade children and read it to the point at which Little Red discovers that the wolf instead of Grandmother is in the bedroom. Interested in encouraging her children in problem-solving abilities, the teacher asked the children: "How else could the story end?" Though the children all knew the traditional ending, they had no difficulty in solving the problem in other ways. Among the stories they wrote were these:

Little Red Riding Hood came out of the cottage. Then she bumped into a fisherman going to a lake. Then the wolf began to run away. Grandmother could feel the wolf's heart go thump, thump. She could also feel the wolf's ribs, veins, and bones. The fisherman knew just what to do. He got his fishing pole, and threw it. The hook caught the wolf and

[4] An unusual version of this tale is by Nonny Hogrogian, *The Renowned History of Little Red Riding Hood.* In this version both Granny and the ingenuous Red come to a mournful end.

stopped him. Grandmother walked out. And they had goodies for lunch.

by Greg

Little Red Riding Hood came screaming out of the cottage, yelling: "Wolf, wolf!" She met the forest ranger, and said, "Oh, Mr. Forest Ranger, please help me." "O.K." he said. They went to the cottage and found the wolf lying on the floor. Two minutes later Grandmother popped out of the wolf's mouth. "How did you do it, Grandmother?" asked Red. "I took karate when I was nineteen, and just socked it to him," said Grandmother.

by Jeff

Little Red Riding Hood ran out of the woods. She ran and ran. She ran about a mile. Then she jumped up in a tree. The wolf couldn't get her. She jumped to another tree, and then another. Her grandmother sure didn't feel well. Then right by the last tree was a little cliff. Little Red Riding Hood jumped on. The wolf climbed up after her. At the top of the cliff Little Red Riding Hood met a hunter. She asked him to kill the wolf, and he did. Then they went to the cottage. They cut open the wolf. The wolf had jumped so much that grandmother had jumped out a long time ago. She came in, and they all ate. And they gave the wolf skin to grandmother.

by Ann

Another folktale, less well known than "Little Red Riding Hood," is equally useful in plot-completion problem solving.

Try reading "Mother Halle"[5] to the point at which lazy Marie plunges into the well. Then let the children write their own conclusions to the tale.

Or take *Anansi, the Spider*[6] and read it to the point at which Anansi is carried into the heavens by the big bird. What is the solution? How will the sons help their father Anansi? Before writing, you might do a brief review of each of the son's abilities and then encourage children to work out their own solutions.

Another plot completion possibility is included in *Swimmy,* an engaging story of an adventuresome little fish, a capable problem solver despite his small size.[7] Read the story to the point at which he declares that something must be done. Then have the children write their own solutions to this problem. Provide an opportunity when the writing is finished for children to share their stories orally, and then read Lionni's ending to them. When some third grade children recently heard the story, they wrote these solutions:

> Then Swimmy thought of an idea. They could find a huge clam shell and hide in it. They could keep it half open and peek.
>
> by Mary

> "I have it," said the youngest fish. "Let's go to the president of the fish. He is right over there at that

[5] Included in Wanda Gag, ed. and trans., *More Tales from Grimm,* pp. 15–22. A very patterned plot, contrasting an industrious, good-willed character with a lazy, ill-tempered one, the story has illustrations in Gag's easily identifiable style.

[6] Gerald McDermott, ed. and illustrator, *Anansi, the Spider.* The vibrantly colored illustrations, highly stylized with bold geometric patterns, enhance the Ashanti tale from Ghana.

[7] Leo Lionni, *Swimmy.* One of the strong points of the book is the illustrations: sophisticated and stylish collages using paint, paper, and stamping techniques in imaginative ways.

boat." So they went. They held a fish conference. The president said, "We will build a sub that will have radar, and we'll go to the flying fish that will bomb the big fish with octopus fluids." It worked, so they had a party.

by Jeff

Swimmy said, "I got it." Then he swam away. Meanwhile the red fish looked puzzled. Swimmy went to the eel and asked, "Will you come and protect us?" The eel answered, "Yes." Then he went to the lobster and asked, "Will you come and protect us?" The lobster answered, "Yes." Then Swimmy went back, and the fish started to swim. On the way they met the big red fish. All of a sudden, the eel came and hit the big fish with his tail. Then came the lobster and punched the big fish to death. And the little fish swam freely.

by Greg

PLOT CREATION

Children should have experiences with three types of plot creation problems. In the first of these, children are asked to extend the story *backward in time*. The teacher reads a story to children, and then encourages them to speculate on what happened before the story began.

A group of first graders recently enjoyed hearing "Cinderella." [8] They then were asked to think about what happened before the story began. The teacher used such questions as these to encourage a free flow of ideas:

---

[8] This teacher used the version by Beni Montresor. Rich in detail omitted in other versions, this one is lavishly, if darkly, illustrated.

- What was Cinderella's father like?
- Where had he, Cinderella, and her mother lived before the mother died?
- How did the mother die?
- How long ago did this happen?
- Where and how did Cinderella's father meet his new wife?

After being encouraged to speculate on answers to these and other questions, children dictated their versions of the events up to the time the familiar version begins.

Another type of plot problem is to extend the story *forward in time*. Children can listen to a story, and then through skillful questioning the teacher can motivate them to write about what happened after the conclusion of the story as the author wrote it.

In the preceding examples, part of a story was read to children, who were then asked to complete it using their own ideas. In this writing experience, the teacher reads the entire book, which has a very equivocal ending.[9] Theodore, in despair because his friends have found out about his duplicity, runs away. Lionni ends the story here, though children may wonder about the fate of Theodore. Try reading the story to children and then ask them to speculate on what happened to Theodore after the story ended. Following such an experience, intermediate grade children wrote the following stories. In many of the stories, Theodore did find new friends to take the place of those he lost because he was so foolish. For example:

Theodore ran all the way to Wisconsin, where he made his home in a beaver hut. One night when Theodore was looking around, he saw a beaver coming toward him. He hid in a little hole. When

[9] Leo Lionni, *Theodore and the Talking Mushroom.*

the beaver was inside, Theodore decided to try to get out. He climbed out, and crept towards the opening. "Hello," said the beaver. "Hi," said Theodore in a faint voice. "What's your name?" asked the beaver. "Theodore," he said. "My name is Barney. Let's be friends." Theodore said, "O.K." Theodore told him about his old friends. "Okay, now it's my turn to show you some of my friends. This is Dana Doe." "Hi Dana," said Theodore. "This is Bopp Bear." "Hi, Bopp." "Hi," he said in a low voice.

One night Theodore was sleeping, and thinking of what kind of friends he had met. They were nice, kind, and thoughtful. Theodore had changed very much, because he was around nice people.

by Joe

Theodore ran all the way to the Gulf of Mexico. He got on a ship going to Brazil. No sooner had the ship landed than Theodore found a friend. His friend was a wolf, whose name was Wolfy. Theodore got on Wolfy's back. He was taking Theodore to his friend, Mr. Owl.

When Mr. Owl saw Theodore, he dove down at Theodore. It was a close call. Mr. Owl just missed Theodore. "Don't hurt Theodore. He's my friend," said Wolfy. "Would you like to be my friend, too?" asked Theodore. "No! What makes you think I'll be a rodent's friend?"

So Wolfy took Theodore to a snake. His name was Snake-eye-Sidney, called Sid, for short. Sid liked nice plump, juicy rodents for supper, but Theodore was a skinny, unflavored rodent. "Sid, will you be my friend?" asked Theodore. "Why sure. Just don't get nice and plump and juicy."

So Sid, Wolfy, and Theodore lived happily until Theodore got nice, plump, and juicy.

by James

Theodore ran and ran until he collapsed. When he looked around he found himself near a small stream. He also found that it was almost dark. Theodore didn't know what to do. Should he look for someone, or just stay there until morning? He was thinking about it when suddenly a cricket chirped. He ran to an old tree stump. Shivering, he looked around. In the dark he thought he saw a shape in the corner. Then he whispered, "Are you there?"

"Yes," said a low-pitched voice. "Who are you?" Theodore asked, gaining courage. "I'm Tom, the Toad," said the voice, "and I live here." "I'm very sorry about this," Theodore said, "but I'm new here." "By the way, what's your name?" asked Tom. "Oh, I'm Theodore. I just got here, and I'm looking for a home." "You could live with me," said Tom. "That's very nice of you. I think I will," Theodore concluded. The two new friends sat there talking for a while. Later on they both went to sleep. When they woke up, Theodore said, "Ever since I met you, I've gained confidence in myself. I like you."

by Roger

Theodore kept running, running, running. Then he saw a hole to hide in, because his friends were trailing right behind him. So he went down the hole. He thought it would be the beginning of a new life. He saw some of his own kind, a mother mouse, and an old Grandmother mouse. She was very old, in her 90's. She had a shawl on her shoulders, and wore spectacles. The Grandmother mouse saw Theodore, and said, "Come in, Sonny, come in. We always welcome visitors." So he came in. That family had always wanted a little boy, but they never had one, so they were very happy to see him. They gave him some supper, and then he went to bed. And in the morning the family wanted him so badly that they adopted him.

by Chrissy

Children most commonly provided Theodore with new animal friends. In the story that follows, Theodore's new friends are people and dolls.

Famished and lonely, Theodore went hunting for food. Then he smelled a funny scent. As he followed the scent he came up to a log cabin. Not looking, Theodore put his head in the cabin. When he looked in the window, he saw two finely crusted pies. Theodore was so hungry he would try anything for those pies. He climbed in the window, and onto the table. The pies were just sitting there. He was just about to take a bite out of the luscious looking pies when all of a sudden Miss Betty Thomas came into the kitchen, holding two dolls called Rebecca and Annabelle. Her mother was following with two dolls, Ruth and Francis. Well, getting back to Theodore, he frighteningly dived into the pies. Betty seeing him do so, pulled him out, and they became friends. Theodore lived at the log cabin with Betty, her mother, Rebecca, Annabelle, Ruth and Francis for evermore.

by Jody

In the case of the last story from this particular writing assignment, Theodore does find happiness of a temporary nature with a blue mushroom strangely reminiscent of those he knew before he ran away. Final happiness comes, however, with an interesting metamorphosis quite unusual in children's writing.

Theodore had stopped running. He was lonely as he looked around. He couldn't see anything familiar. Theodore decided to go to the top of the hill and look around. It took a long time because he was tired. Finally the mouse got there.

All of a sudden he heard a long "Quirp." He heard it again and again. Suddenly he recognized it. He looked around and around and around. Then he saw it. It was a blue mushroom. He ran down the hill, and ran, and ran, and ran, until he got to the mushroom. He was happy to see the blue mushroom. "Quirp, Quirp," said the mushroom. "Quirp, Quirp." Theodore fell asleep. When he woke up it was dark outside. Theodore missed his friends very much. He missed cuddling up and sleeping with them. He couldn't go to sleep again because he was so lonely.

In the morning Theodore woke up and went out in the wood to get some food. He succeeded, and went back to the blue mushroom. "I can't call you blue mushroom all the time," said Theodore. "I'll have to give you a name." Theodore thought and thought and thought and finally he decided. "I will name you Melvin!" Theodore said.

Theodore was happy now that he had Melvin (Quirp) and Melvin had him. For many days Theodore stayed with Melvin and they were happy. One day Theodore woke up with a funny feeling.

He felt very sick. The whole day he stayed under Melvin. A day passed, and another day, and every day he felt sicker and sicker. The next morning he woke up. He felt different. He felt better. He looked around. He wasn't under Melvin anymore. He could not bend. Something had happened. He tried to talk, but all he could say was, "Quirp, Quirp." Now he knew. He had turned into a blue mushroom.

by Ginny

Another opportunity to extend plot forward in time is provided in the exciting episodic adventures of Cary, Charles, and Paul.[10] A teacher read this book to a group of third grade children, who were disappointed at the completion of the book that the adventures had come to an end. The teacher then asked them to create another adventure for the children. The following stories are typical of those the children wrote. The first is especially interesting because the writer chose to use first person narration.

The ride was fun. It wasn't long. I almost fell off, but Carey caught me. Finally we got there. We saw two dinosaurs fighting. We also met some cave men who were roaming around. A dinosaur tried to get us, but I quickly turned the bedknob and we got away. We came down.

We ate with the cavemen. Then Paul and Charles went to look around with the cave man's little boy. Carey and I stayed, and learned about living with so many dinosaurs around. We had lots of fun, but then the king of the dinosaurs came. Quickly we all jumped on the bed. We yelled, "Good-bye." Then the dinosaur chased us but we flew down

[10] Mary Norton, *Bedknob and Broomstick*.

very fast and escaped. Then we went home and jumped in bed.

by Kathy

One day Paul said, "I would like to go into the past, wouldn't you? Then we could see ourselves when we were young." "Heh, heh. That would be good." So they turned the knob. The bed moved very fast.

They arrived at a big mansion. They said, "Wow. Is that mother's house?" "I, I guess so." "It's awfully big," said Paul.

Then Carey said, "Let's quit gabbing about the house, and see our mother and ourselves when we were young!" They opened the big white door. Then Carey said, "They can't see us." "Good," Paul blurted out. They saw two maids holding Charles and Paul as babies. Carey toddled all around the house. Then they got in the bed, and went home.

by Erika

After they got back, it was Charles' turn to choose. "I think I'll go to Africa." O.K.," said Carey. "Let's go now," cried Paul. So off they went. On the way they passed an airplane. "Look," said a boy on the plane, "a flying bed." "Nonsense." "But—" "But nothing." So away they flew.

When they reached Africa they landed in the water. Then they swam to shore. And at the shore there was a tiger, so they ran as fast as an automobile. But the tiger ran faster. Just as the tiger was going to get them, they ran into a mob of zebras. The tiger's mouth was open so wide that he ate a rock. He was so full he couldn't run. Paul was so afraid that he started to cry.

When they reached the shore, there were elephants on the bed. So they sat on the shore until midnight. Then the elephants left. Finally the children got the bed, and went away. When they got home they went to sleep, and never went there again.

by Paul

A third type of plot problem asks children to set the story in another place, or another time. In the story, *The Bat Poet*,[11] the author has set the story in the country. Several of the problems the bat encounters are caused because of dangers unique to the setting. When the setting is changed, some of the problems change. Groups of children have found it an exciting challenge to write an adventure for the bat while on a visit to the city.

Three days later the little brown bat found himself in Los Angeles. He was walking along, reciting a poem as he was going. Suddenly a rough bearded man ran up to the then frightened bat, and said, "My gosh, you're terrific!"

This man's name was Franklin Pants. He was the owner of Poet's Anonymous. He then pulled out a contract and asked the fluffy animal to sign it. The brown bat thought to himself, and signed.

Months went by, and the star wrote many books. One book he wrote was called, *I Used to be a Country Hang Down*. He even got to meet the president. This was the life. But for a *bat*?

by Andy

11 Randall Jarrell, *The Bat Poet*.

After Brown Bat left his friends, he went flying for three days. He finally saw a huge city. He thought to himself, "Wow! I'll bet that city will be a blast."

So he went flying to the city. When he got there he saw cars, trucks, buildings, and houses. He saw a house that had a window open, and he flew in the window. He saw a lady, and the lady saw him. The lady screamed (naturally!) and called the police. Brown Bat got so scared he flew out the window.

He was flying around some more, and saw a man's car that had a broken windshield. So he flew in the car. The man saw him, and said, "Oh, not a bat." The man took his windshield wiper that had fallen off his car, and threw it at Brown Bat. Luckily, it missed. So he flew out of the man's car in a hurry, and said to himself. "This city's not for me. I think I'll go back home. Right away!" So he flew back home.

by Ellen

One day little brown bat decided to visit the city. The next night he started out. Since there was a city quite near, he got there by dawn. Little brown bat did not know where to go in the big city. So he flew into the first window he saw.

Luckily the window was open, and even more luckily it was the window of Amelia R. Hortan, an animal lover. Amelia had three dogs, three cats, and a couple of bunnies, not to mention the fifteen others that ran through the house.

The brown bat was lucky because Amelia was looking for a new pet to add to her collection of animals. So, when the little brown bat flew through the window, she was delighted, and immediately went up to the attic to get a cage for little brown bat. Little brown bat liked it at Amelia's house, but he wanted to go back to the country. After a while, Amelia decided to take the little brown bat to the country. The next day he was back in the country.

by Sylvia

One student set her story in two different locations:

The bat went to the desert, and he met an owl. The owl's name was Fred, and he was very nice. The bat was flying along and he hit a cactus. He got a needle from the cactus in his wing. He thought it hurt like having his wing cut off. Then Fred came and flew him to the animal hospital. The bat looked down, saw all the cars, and thought that they looked like big monsters with flashing eyes. The owl told him he was in the city. The doctor pulled the needle out and put a bandage on his wing. The bat decided to stay in the city with the owl. They got married and lived happily ever after.

by Susie

The little brown bat was in the city now. He had come to the city to try it out. He knew he had to find a home first—a home which had a plentiful food supply, including water and, of course, good shelter. The second thing the little brown bat had to consider was how rough-and-rugged it would be in the city. He also had to find out what he would do in his spare time. He was a good writer—more of a poet—but would he have things to write about?

Would he have time? The answers to these questions and more he could only find out in time.

The little brown bat just spotted a very little cubbyhole under a house roof. It was good enough for him, and he decided that that was his house, his home.

The next day was probably the worst day of his life. He couldn't find food or water. He went the entire day without any meals. The next day was so bad the little brown bat decided to leave. So far he was so busy and unsuccessful he didn't write any poems. He just couldn't take life in the city. The situation was getting worse and worse.

Two days later the little brown bat left. He went back to the country. Back to his friends. Back to peace. Back to writing. That bat never went back to the city. He wrote and wrote and wrote until he died of old age. He had lived a good life.

by Andy

Zero is a bat who had many adventures. This story is one of them. Zero was never allowed to go into the city called Gemini. One day a tornado came and swept the bat family out of its house. The mother and father died, but Zero lived. Zero could not figure out where he was. Then he remembered. There were tall buildings, and lots of cars and people. This was the big city, Gemini.

Zero wandered around for a while, until he came to a church. He saw a big bell at the top. He flew into the bell, and all of a sudden the bell started to rock. The bell made the biggest noise Zero had ever heard.

Down below there was a parade going on in honor of the new mayor. There were bands and floats. Zero liked this, so he flew down to one of the bands. Accidentally he flew into a tuba.

Lots of people saw this and they screamed. Everyone ran away from the parade. Just then, another tornado came. It swept Zero back to the country. Zero found a new mother and father, and they lived happily ever after.

by Peter

PLOT AND THE FABLE

All of the foregoing writing experiences are ways of providing a facilitating structure within which children can work. Another form, or genre, which can be used effectively is the fable.[12] Fables featuring animal characters are brief and lead to an explicitly stated moral. A group of intermediate grade teachers used a book by Galdone to introduce the form to their children.[13] Following the reading of the fables, children were asked to take one of the morals and write another fable that would illustrate the moral. The following were written for the moral: *Never trust a flatterer.*

Once upon a time there was a rabbit and a squirrel. The squirrel said that the rabbit was a very good jumper. One day the squirrel asked the rabbit if he could jump over the creek. The rabbit said if there was mud on the creek bottom he wouldn't jump, because he might get stuck in the mud. Before the squirrel asked the rabbit, he had put

[12] Suggestions by other authors about fables are included in Eldonna Evertts, "Dinosaurs, Witches and Anti-Aircraft: Primary Composition," in *Language and Language Arts,* ed. Johanna S. DeStefano and Sharon E. Fox, pp. 387–395. Or see Paul C. Burns et al., "Written Composition," in *The Language Arts in Childhood Education,* pp. 182–247.

[13] Paul Galdone, *Three Aesop Fox Fables.*

nuts on the bottom of the creek. Then the squirrel walked across the creek on the nuts. Then the rabbit jumped across the creek, and he didn't go all the way. He got stuck in the mud. The squirrel left, and Mr. Fox came and ate the rabbit up.

by Fred

One day a new bird moved into the forest. Her name was Vicky Chickedy. When she met Patty Peacock she thought that Patty was the most beautiful bird in the world. She told Patty how beautiful she was. Vicky gave Patty all sorts of impressive comments. Vicky also liked Patty's husband, Micky Chicky, too. She said Patty should enter the beauty contest. Patty soon left for the beauty contest. When she came back, she couldn't find Micky or Vicky. She found out that they ran off, and got married.

by Doug

One day a weasle was walking in the forest. He hadn't eaten in two days. All of a sudden he saw a farm . . . with Hens! He saw some eggs being guarded by a very ugly hen. The weasle walked up to the hen and said, "How beautiful you are, my sweet hen."

"Don't kid me," the hen said. "I know all you want are the eggs!"

"Oh, my fair lady, go look in the mirror if you don't believe me," said the weasle.

"Do you really mean it? Really and truly, I'm beautiful?" asked the hen. "Yes!" nodded the weasle. And off went the ugly hen to look in the mirror. When she got back all the eggs were gone.

by Wendy

Several of the children chose to write a fable for the moral: *Tricksters cannot complain when they in return are tricked.*

"Hello, Coyote," said the Roadrunner.

"Today I've got a surprise for you. Just wait," said the coyote. Meanwhile the coyote dug a deep hole where they were going to race. Then he covered it with sticks and grass. He figured that the roadrunner would race on the left side, and fall in the hole so he could win the race. But as he was going to the starting line, he forgot which side the hole was on, so he decided to race on the left side.

"You say you're going to beat me," said the roadrunner.

"Yes," said the coyote.

The race began. The roadrunner was in the lead. All of a sudden the coyote fell in the hole, and the roadrunner won the race.

by Geri

Once there was a cat and a ferret who were good friends. The cat said to the ferret, "If you get me a plump, fat, juicy mouse, I'll get you a fish." So the ferret went off, and came to a mouse. The ferret said, "Do you want to play a game?" The mouse said, "O.K.," so they went to play. The ferret hid. The mouse went looking for the ferret. The mouse passed the ferret, and then the ferret grabbed the mouse. The mouse said, "Let me go." "No," said the ferret. So the ferret took the mouse to the cat. The ferret asked, "Where is my fish?" The cat replied, "Go find your own fish."

by Dawn

The third fable in the Galdone book also interested several of the children. In the following example, the writer incorporated the moral into the fable.

> The dog was going to give a party. He invited the rabbit, the frog, and the cow. They were all very good friends. When they arrived at the dog's house, the dog hadn't yet decided what to eat. The dog suggested beef burgers. The rabbit strongly protested. He said carrots. The dog hesitated, but agreed. The frog said if they were having carrots he would leave. He wanted bugs. The cow said if they were having bugs *or* carrots he would leave and no longer be the dog's friend. They argued, all but the dog. He got them quieted down and said: *Please all and you will please none.*
>
> by Katy

There was once a little donkey who lived in an old shabby house all by himself. One day he decided to paint his house because it was so old and shabby looking. So he went out to the store to buy some paint. He decided on gray, because of his skin color. He got home and started to paint. Right after he finished painting and got down from the ladder, along came his friend, the tiger. The donkey welcomed his guest, and mentioned the painting of his house. The tiger said it looked all right, but that he had painted the house all wrong. He said the donkey should have painted it orange with black stripes. The donkey agreed, and went out to buy orange and black paint.

He went home and started to paint. When he finished, along came his friend the zebra. The zebra said he liked the donkey's house, but he should have painted it white with black stripes.

So the donkey went out and bought more paint and repainted the house. Now he was getting angry, so he sat down to rest. He was confused and tired. He was getting a little sleepy, when along came his friend, the lion. The lion said he definitely hated the donkey's painting job, and told the donkey he should have painted the house yellow with a touch of brown. So the donkey got more paint and repainted his house. This happened over and over again, until the donkey had no money left. His house was gray, orange, black, white, yellow, brown, red, and many other colors. He did not like it at all, so finally he moved away, very sad and very broke—with no house!

by Karen

CHARACTER AND PLOT

In helping children develop the ability to write convincing plots, we turn their attention at times to characterization for a consideration of the way changes in characters may affect plot. For example, we may ask children to take a minor character and develop it so the person has more effect on what happens in the story. In a book by Norton, two minor characters, Aunt Beatrice and the maid Agnes, have little effect on the story line. Some inventive child could build either of them into real, functioning characters who actually become significant in changing the flow of the plot.[14]

In addition to increasing the importance of a minor character, we sometimes ask children to *add* a character to the story for the effect this has on plot. This technique is de-

[14] Norton, *Bedknob and Broomstick.* Further discussion of the idea of character expansion is included in John Warren Stewig, *Spontaneous Drama.*

scribed here, rather than in the chapter on characterization, since the focus is on the *effect* of the new character, not on developing a convincing character as in chapter three. Having created such a character, the children must logically weave the character into the action.

Intermediate grade teachers have had success in introducing this idea to children by using a favorite story by Dahl.[15] They read the story to the point at which the fifth ticket had been found, and then asked children:

- If there was a sixth ticket, who would get it?
- What kind of person would he/she be?
- How would he/she fit into the story?
- How might the story change if there were another person?

Following such introduction and discussion, fifth and sixth grade children recently wrote the following descriptions. Some of these were quite brief, yet provided enough substance for their creators to weave them into the story action.

The winner of the sixth golden ticket is Daffleduff Dirt. The reporters showed a close-up view of him. He was sitting there waving the golden ticket that was covered with dust and all kinds of other dirt. His parents were standing ten feet away from him, because they were ashamed of him. He was sitting there grinning, and saying, "I have broken the world's record for not taking a bath. I haven't taken a bath in one whole year! I have so much dirt on me now that I can grow carrots and beets on my arms. People always say that I have a green arm. My Mom is always asking me to take a bath,

---

[15] Roald Dahl, *Charlie and the Chocolate Factory.*

but I keep on saying that I want to break the world's record, and it will ruin my garden."

by Brenda

Alicia Alta Anderson entered "Patricia's Pub." She sat down, and in her most lady-like voice said, "I will have vodka. And a Wonka bar." (She said this softly, because *nobody* eats chocolate in a bar!) Alicia thought to herself, "What great publicity I would have if I got the golden ticket." She opened the bar, quite calmly for that matter. "You have the golden ticket," said Patricia. "So I do." And with that Alicia proudly but snobbishly left.

Facts about Alicia:

Hair—long, ebony black

Eyes—creamy brown

Height—5'10"

Weight—125

Age—21

Home—Paris

Occupation—Model

by Debbie

Another example, quite completely developed, includes a carefully thought-out bridge between Dahl's story and the author's writing. It provides a wealth of detail, not only about the new character, but also about the way in which the golden ticket was found.

The fifth ticket was gone with one ticket left. So far the lucky people were August Bloop, Veruca Salt, Mike Teavee, Violet Beauregarde, and Charlie Bucket. There would be one more lucky person, and they would be very lucky because tomorrow would be the big day at the Chocolate Factory.

It was early. So early that the only thing you could hear was the rustling of chocolate candy bars being unwrapped. This sound you could hear all around the town. Then suddenly there was a scream, "I got it! I got it, I got it, I got the golden ticket. Weeeeee—Whoopee!"

And out of nowhere comes these high pigtails that were golden red, and this face that was covered with freckles. Then the rest of her came out. She had a lollypop in one hand, and a golden ticket in the other. Her name was Freakela Lolly Goldenred. Her nickname was Freckles. She was a thin girl and lived on the east side of town.

Later that morning everybody was excited, happy, and some were mad. Just before the time to go, Freakela explained the story to the newsmen. When she heard they were having a contest, she was so mad because it wasn't with lollypops, and after a while she said, "You can't always win." So she went and bought five candy bars, because five was her lucky number. She said, "What happened was that I got the golden ticket on the third bar, so now three is my lucky number."

That day she was dressed in a dress with lollypops on them. She also had on pink shoes. She looked rather pretty, except for the stickiness of the lollypop she had in her hand. Her big sister was taking her to the Chocolate Factory. Her sister's name was Pimpla, because of her pimples. Finally, it was time, so off they went to the chocolate factory.

by Jerilyn

Following this initial experience in character creation, the teachers read the remainder of the story to the children.

The children's writing task then was to retell the story in their own words, incorporating their character. Several days of writing were necessary and resulted in extended stories of fifteen to twenty pages in length—an impressive writing project for intermediate grade children.

Many books for children offer similar opportunities for character addition. Your children might enjoy a delightful rhymed fantasy by Berg.[16] In the story the main character solves a seemingly unsolvable problem by using her roller skating hobby, thus winning the king's reward. Tessie is a rugged individualist, but that doesn't negate the value of having children consider: Who else could help Tessie solve the king's dusty and dirty problem?

Another character addition possibility exists in *What's the Matter With Carruthers?*, an animal fantasy with much appeal for young children.[17] Emily and Eugene, friends of the lethargic bear Carruthers, indeed do need help in their attempts to restore cranky Carruthers to his former amiable self. Who could help them? Posing this question to a group of children and having them create a character who would influence the direction of the plot is sure to result in some effective writing.

A more sophisticated problem, probably best reserved for upper grade children, is to attempt placing a story in another time. Children enjoy taking a fairy tale and changing it to fit life today. This results in more than plot changes, for some elements of setting and characterization will need to be changed.

One group of fourth grade children with whom I worked was going to write a version of "Little Red" to share with some first graders. In retelling the story, the class became concerned with how she could be so gullible, so oblivious to obvious danger signals, so the group decided to develop

16 Jean Horton Berg, *Miss Tessie Tate.*
17 James Marshall, *What's the Matter with Carruthers?*

a characterization of a slightly more perspicacious Little Red. The devious wolf had a much more difficult job in our adapted version of the tale, when Little Red took on some of the sophistication natural to the space-age children who were composing the story.

SEQUENCE IN PLOT

Children assume—and most often we reinforce the idea—that in composing, the writer begins at the beginning and goes in a relatively straight line to the end. This is a logical assumption, since the vast majority of stories for children are constructed this way. Nonetheless, it may be useful, particularly with older children, to explore other options.

One pair of authors suggests having children experiment with:

- beginning at the end of a story and then going back to the beginning
- beginning at the middle of the story and then returning to the actual beginning [18]

An effective way to introduce this idea to children would be to share a book by Neville with them.[19] In the book chapters one and fifteen are set in New York City; the time is the present. The remainder of the book is an extended flashback to Berries's life several years earlier in rural New York State. Another book helpful for this purpose is by Henry.[20]

[18] Harry A. Greene and Walter T. Petty, *Developing Language Skills in the Elementary Schools,* p. 307.
[19] Emily C. Neville, *Berries Goodman.*
[20] Marguerite Henry, *Justin Morgan Had a Horse.*

TYPES OF CONFLICT

The element that most often makes writing interesting is conflict. Effective descriptions, convincing characters, and sprightly dialogue do not hold our interest for long unless the author creates some sort of conflict. For a plot to develop in exciting fashion, the author must develop a conflict. Thus, in helping children become better writers, we must help them understand conflict and how to create it.

Writers have identified three types of conflict; examples of all three types are found in literature for children. First, there is the conflict of *person versus person*, in which two approximately equal forces desire different things. An example of this type is the conflict between the title characters in "The Fisherman and His Wife." [21]

A second type of conflict is *person versus fate*, i.e., the individual versus nature, the supernatural, or something larger than himself/herself. In this case, it is two unequal forces opposing each other. An example of this type is found in the old Italian folktale about the overly confident shepherd.[22] The wily shepherd contends against the stronger force, the month, but finally loses.

In the third type of conflict, *individual versus self*, an internal flaw in the character creates the problem. This time it is not external forces, but rather the nature of the character that results in the conflict. An example of this type is the tale of the willful chick whose callous indifference to the needs of others eventually leads to its downfall.[23]

[21] In the folktale section of May Hill Arbuthnot, *Arbuthnot Anthology of Children's Literature*, p. 288. This is also available in *Chimney Corner Fairy Tales* by Veronica S. Hutchinson. The versions included are embellished with black and white drawings, and with full color illustrations by Lois Lenski in her easily identifiable style. The colors are pastel, the designs highly patterned into stylized views of a world very unlike our own.

[22] May Hill Arbuthnot, *Arbuthnot Anthology of Children's Literature*.

[23] Veronica S. Hutchinson, *Chimney Corner Fairy Tales*.

TYPE-ONE CONFLICT

Children can be helped to develop skill in writing stories incorporating each of the three types of conflict. One first grade teacher was working on the idea of conflict as an element in stories. When studying type one, *person versus person*, her children dictated the following stories of conflict, illustrating two people of approximately equal status desiring different things.

> I have ten cents. I'm buying ice cream. Chocolate. My sister wants strawberry. We argue. So we don't get ice cream; we get bubble gum.
>
> by Danny

> I had an argument with my friend. I wanted her to come to my house, and she wanted me to go to her house. So neither one of us went anywhere.
>
> by Rachel

> One day I went to my room and got one dollar. I wanted to go to the store. My mom said, "If you want to go, your sister goes, too." "O.K.," I said. "What do you want to get?" She wanted a doll. I wanted a car. I said, "You can't spend my money on a doll. Go to Mom and you can use her money." So she did.
>
> by Keither

A first grade child wrote the following story about animals, based on a type-one conflict.

> My dog Fluffy grabbed our kitten's ball of yarn, and the kitten grabbed Fluffy's toy ball. Then a big

conflict started. After a while a cardinal came. The kitten ran after it. It was gone! My dog gave the kitten the yarn. Fluffy helped the kitten catch the bird, so the kitten gave Fluffy his ball. They made up and played happily ever after.

by Julie

Intermediate grade children can also benefit from a study of type-one conflict. After reading several stories illustrating this type of conflict, fifth and sixth grade children wrote the following stories. In the first example, the writer borrowed character names from a popular television series and developed a realistically treated conflict.

It was a bright, sunny morning. Jodi was all set to go to baseball practice.

"Uncle Bill, do you know where Buffy is?" asked Jodi.

"Well, you know Buffy—she always seems to take longer than you do," laughed Uncle Bill.

"Then will you tell Buffy to meet me down at the park?" asked Jodi.

"Sure," said Uncle Bill.

Meanwhile, Jodi walked down to the park, and saw the team waiting.

"Buffy will be right down," said Jodi.

"Listen, Jodi, I'm the captain of this team, and I don't want to have your sister on my team. If there are any objections, just hand in your uniform!" said Tom.

"But here comes Buffy. What are you going to say to her?" asked Jodi.

"Not me. You're the one that's going to tell her. Oh, and practice is at 12:30, if you don't stick up

for your sister!" said Tom as he turned to walk
away.

"What was that all about, and why do you look
so sad?" asked Buffy.

"The boys said you couldn't be on the team, because they don't want girls on the team. They also
said that if you are on their team, I can't be," said
Jodi.

"How about if we form our own team?" asked
Buffy.

"Great idea! Let's go find some girls and boys
to make two teams!" said Jodi.

by Geri

In the following two stories the authors set the story in
an indeterminate past time to allow for a fantasy development of the plot. In the first, a common motif from fairy
tales, a mistreated younger sister, is incorporated into the
action.

Once upon a time, about one hundred years ago,
there lived three sisters and a dog. The dog's name
was Muffles, and the three sister's names were Alice,
Dorothy and Gretle.

About ten years before, Alice, Dorothy and
Gretle's parents died. Since they had no relatives,
Dorothy and Alice were left to raise Gretle alone.
Ten years had now passed and Alice was now 31,
Dorothy was now 30, and Gretle was now 13.

As Gretle grew up, she grew smarter, stronger,
and prettier each day. This made both Alice and
Dorothy jealous. So by giving Gretle all the work
to do, they felt better. Though as Gretle grew up,
despite all her goodness, she did have a bad temper.
Her bad temper only occurred when she had to give

something up. Alice and Dorothy told Gretle that they had to do the very same work when they were thirteen years old.

One warm day in June, as lazy Alice sat beside a window looking at the shiny, red, plump apples, she decided she just must have one. So she called Gretle and said, "Gretle dear, I'm hungry. Please go outside, and climb the apple tree and find the fattest, reddest apple.

"Well," said Gretle, "You look fine to me. So why don't you get your own apple?"

"Well, I don't feel good," (which was a lie Alice made up) "and if you don't," Alice said, raising her voice, "I'll make you."

"Oh, you must really feel bad," interrupted Gretle. "Your temper is worse than mine, so I will go outside and get you an apple."

Gretle finished washing the dishes, put Muffles on a leash, and walked outside. She circled around a stone, and then looked up at the apple tree. Those were the reddest apples Gretle had ever seen. As she looked up at the tree, she spotted at the very top the reddest, shiniest, roundest apple in the world. Gretle intended to get it.

So Gretle started to climb the tree. It was easy for Gretle to climb the tree, though it did get harder as she went up. She reached as high as she could with her small, slender hand, and finally —pluck! The apple fell to the ground. Gretle climbed down to the ground as fast as she could, picked up the apple, and wiped it on her apron.

Just as she started running into the house, she heard a voice which said, "Run away, run away."

"Who said that?" asked Gretle.

"Me," replied the apple. And then the apple

told Gretle that Alice and Dorothy were taking advantage of her because she was so young and strong. After listening to this for quite a while, Gretle was convinced. She decided she would run away with Muffles.

"Except," asked Gretle, "why are you telling me this?"

"I just don't want to be eaten. Since I told you this, you will see to it that I'm not eaten by anyone, won't you?"

"Why, of course, but you still didn't answer my question. Why are you telling me this?" asked Gretle.

"I've been here for five years, and couldn't tell anyone anything until they picked me off this tree. Since you were the one who took me off this tree, I will give you one wish," said the apple.

There were so many other questions Gretle wanted to ask. But as she turned around, she saw Dorothy and Alice coming out, each yelling, "I want that apple to eat." Gretle refused to give Alice and Dorothy the apple. Dorothy and Alice started wishing for things but nothing happened.

Finally Gretle got very mad and she said, "I wish Dorothy and Alice would leave and never come back again." As she looked, she couldn't believe her eyes, for there where Alice and Dorothy were, was nothing.

She searched the house and couldn't find either Dorothy or Alice. Muffles was happy. The apple was very happy, and Gretle was the happiest of all. They all lived happily ever after, except Alice and Dorothy.

by Mary

In the following story, two sisters of equal status but with very different natures, finally work out a solution to their problem.

Once two old ladies lived together in a cottage. One was neat and one was messy. One did the house work, and the other took care of the field. The one that took care of the house was the neat one. And the messy one took care of the field.

After work in the field, the one old lady would come in and throw her things all over. The neat sister would make her clean it up. Then the messy sister took her things in her bedroom and put them all in a heap. Then in the morning, the clean sister saw the clothes in a heap. She woke the messy sister up, and told her to clean the mess up. The messy sister said she wouldn't, because it wasn't her job doing the house work. So the clean sister put the clothes away, and cleaned up the messy sister's room.

That day was the messy sister's day off, and she didn't have to go to the field. So the clean sister snuck out to see how the field was doing. She got a big shock. There was no plowed field. It was just a piece of land. She ran home and got the messy sister up. She made her go to the piece of land, and make the field of vegetables.

But the house was clean, so the clean sister went to see how well the field was doing. But all she saw was the piece of land. She didn't see her messy sister, so she started to look for her. She looked for about half an hour. Then she found her sister lying under a pear tree eating pears and throwing the pear cores around. Now the clean sister was very mad, and was so mad she felt like kicking her messy sister out.

So she made a plan. She said to herself, "I will tell her that if she hasn't plowed the land she will have to move."

So when the messy sister got home, she threw her dirty clothes on the chair. They really weren't very dirty, but the messy sister threw them in the mud on the way home.

"Well," said the clean sister, "let's go see how the field is coming."

"No," said the messy sister.

"Why?" asked the clean sister.

"Because you might not think it's O.K."

"I'll bet you're just trying to keep me away from it," said the clean sister.

"Alright, alright. I didn't do the field."

"Then you're moving. You never do any work."

So the dirty sister moved, and they both lived happily ever after.

by Kathy

TYPE-TWO CONFLICT

Understanding of *type-two conflict* is more difficult to develop with children but is worth working on nonetheless. Because the concept is more abstract, the writing that results will tend to be less impressive than that which results from either type one or three. Writing about an individual in conflict with fate, that is, nature, the supernatural, or some force larger than himself/herself, may be difficult for children, but intermediate children can try their hands at it. Children who studied this type of conflict wrote the following stories:

It was a calm, cool April night. I was fishing off the pier near Savannah, Georgia all alone. Suddenly it started to rain. Harder and harder it came down. I picked up all of my tackle and ran for home.

Then, just as suddenly as it had started, it stopped. It was calm again. I knew this meant that a tornado was coming, so I ran even faster toward some caves I had been in before. In the distance I saw the dark, funnel shape of the tornado. "I must make it to the caves," I thought. I was full of panic and fear. It was still at least two hundred feet up to the cave and the tornado was getting very close.

The cave was just a small hole in a thin but high projection of rock. The winds had begun to pick up, and the tornado was even closer, coming straight toward me. The cave was only twenty-five feet away when the tornado hit the beach. Closer and closer it came, but closer and closer I got to the cave.

I had just made it to the cave and gotten in the side room when I saw weeds, trees, and other things flying around. It bounced in front of the cave, and bounced on the other side. How lucky I was! How relieved I felt!

When I got back home there were a few homes completely demolished, but our's wasn't. My parents were so glad to see me that they cried and hugged me. I was just as happy to see them, and I told them so.

by Roger

In the following story, the writer has personified the force—nature as Mrs. Flood bringing judgment on a man

who displeased her. The result is an intriguing piece of
writing with much originality.

Once there was a lady whose name was Mrs.
Flood. She only flooded when she lost her temper.
One day she saw a man shooting at a dog. She lost
her temper. "Oh, boy!" she said. "Is he going to
get it!"

All of a sudden the flood began. Then the man
began to run. But another flood began. He was
trapped! No, he wasn't. He was near a tree. He was
glad he knew how to climb trees.

"Phew," he said. "I'll be safe here, at least for a
while." Then Mrs. Flood saw what he had done.

"Oh, well," she said, "I'll just make it rain very
hard, so it will start lightening." So she made it
start to rain. And then a lot of lightening hit the
tree.

"Crash!" Splash!" Down went the tree. Luckily
the man was on the opposite side of the tree from
the side that was hitting the ground. Then the tree
began to float. The man was so happy.

Then the tree began to sink. "Oh, boy," said the
man. "I'm supposed to know how to swim. Here
goes nothing!" So he began to swim. The water was
98 feet over his head (and he was 6'2"). He could
hold his breath for seven minutes. Then something
blocked his path. It was a huge rock. He went to
the top of the rock. The top of the rock was fifty
feet above the water. Really what the man was
looking at was a very high mountain. In a few
minutes the water got higher. Then the man
looked up at the sky and said, "Oh, Mrs. Flood.
I'm sorry I was shooting at the dog. I'll never do

it again." Then suddenly it was the sunniest day possible.

by Rod

One day Pam and her family wanted to go camping. It was a nice day. They packed all their things and left. When they got to where they wanted to camp, they unpacked and set up the trailer.

They wanted to go swimming, so they put on their swimming suits. When they got to the beach, suddenly it started to rain. They had to get out of the water and get into their clothes.

The rain finally stopped. They went mountain climbing. The rocks were sturdy. But after Pam stepped on one, her brother stepped on it, and he fell down the mountain. Pam knew she had to do something, so she quickly decided she would go down to help him.

When she got down the mountain, she saw that a big rock had fallen on her brother's leg. Pam ran for help. She ran and ran until she came to a thicket. She had a tough time getting through the thicket, but she finally got through it.

Then she walked and walked. Suddenly she saw a house. She went up to the house and knocked on the door. Nobody came to the door, so she knocked again. This time someone came to the door. Right away Pam started to tell the person about her brother. When she finished the man said he would come and try to help.

When they got to where her brother was, Pam's mother and dad were there. They all pulled and pulled until the rock came off Sam's leg. They carried him to the car. Then they took him to the hospital. He had a broken leg. He had a cast on his leg for five months, until his leg got better.

by Mary

TYPE-THREE CONFLICT

Type-three conflict, *individual versus self,* results when problems within the character cause the problem. That is, something in the personality of the character—an internal flaw—results in conflict.

When working on type-three conflict, one kindergarten teacher was trying to help children see that some aspect of their character may make for conflict. The children dictated these descriptions of character traits that might lead to conflict:

> I do naughty things like playing in my mom's drawers. My mom tells me not to, but I do it anyway. I should do what she says because if I don't, I won't get my allowance.
>
> by Debbie

> I like to show off. I show off and try to make people laugh when my Mom and Dad have company. Then I get sent to my room, and I get embarrassed.
>
> by Todd

With these character-trait descriptions as a foundation, the next step would be to have children write a complete story, featuring a main character whose trait led to some type of conflict.

Another kindergarten teacher used "The Emperor's New Clothes" [24] to help children think about type-three conflict.

[24] A version is available designed and illustrated by Virginia L. Burton. The tale is also included in the definitive edition of Andersen: trans., E. C. Haugaard, *Hans Christian Andersen—The Complete Fairy Tales and Stories.*

In the story it is the emperor's gullibility that creates the problem. In the following composition, dictated by a child after hearing Andersen's tale, it is the main character's indecision that creates the problem.

> Mr. Henry has too many shoes. And when he goes to work he doesn't know what shoes to wear, so he lays them out at night. He tries to wear two at a time. He goes to work with two pair of shoes on his feet. So other people at work laugh at him.
>
> by Andy

Indecision is also the character flaw described in the following story:

> There was a girl with too many hats, who was going on a date. She was late because she didn't know what to wear. Her boy friend rang the bell, and said, "What's taking so long?" They went off. She wore all her hats one on top of another.
>
> by Ann

Another possible motivation to help primary grade children think about type-three conflict is a delightful old story by Gag.[25] It is jealousy and laziness that gets the husband, Fritzl, into trouble. Gentle Liesi, his wife, goes along with his calamitous idea to change jobs for a day and accepts stoically the results.

Third grade children, studying type-three conflict with their teacher, wrote the following stories illustrating problems that arise because of some trait in the main character.

> She Forgot Again, Oh Boy!
> There was once a nanny who always forgot where she put things. One day she found out a fair was

25 Wanda Gag, *Gone Is Gone*.

coming. The day had come and she got into her pony cart. But she forgot to lock the door. Oh, Boy! So she got out, and she got her keys out of her pocket and locked the door. Then she put her keys in her pocket again. She said, "My keys could fall out. I had better put them somewhere else. She put them in a flower pot in the barn. She went to the fair, and she had lots of fun. After the fair ended she got in her pony cart and she went home. When she got home she had forgotten where she put her keys. She got very mad! Then she remembered she had put the keys in the barn. She went in the barn and got them. She went to the door, unlocked the door, and she went to sleep.

by Jenny

The Man Who Was Stubborn

One night an old man started to eat dinner. When he was done, he said to himself, "Old Man, who should clean your dishes? Well," said the old man, "I think that a wife should clean the dishes." But he did not have a wife.

Out came a little man from nowhere! It looked exactly like him! The old man said, "Who are you?" "I am your conscience. You should do the dishes. It is not a lady's job. If you do not clean them, you will regret it." Then the little man disappeared.

And the next thing you know, another little man who looked just like him also came. It was his devil! He said, "Don't listen to him. He doesn't do any good, but I'll tell you right from wrong. Don't do the dishes." The devil disappeared also.

The old man had both in mind. He went to bed

and dreamed. The next day he was tired. It seemed every night he dreamed.

One night he took his last dish to have supper. He tried to go to bed to finish the dream, but he couldn't. There are dishes all over: on the bed, sink, EVERYWHERE! "Well," he said, "I'll have to pack my bag." But he couldn't, because the room was a mess. He could not see one thing. All of a sudden it began to rain. I guess you know what's going to happen now. He put all the dishes in a truck, and hopped in. He drove into the front yard. He jumped out of the truck, took his handkerchief, and washed every single dish by hand in the rain. By the time he was finished, his clothes were filthy. He was tired, but he learned to be smart.

by Karen

Teddy, the Bear Who Wouldn't Listen

Once there was a bear named Teddy. Teddy was a good bear. One day Teddy's parents said they were going to the fair. Teddy was very excited. When the day came to go to the fair, Teddy's parents told Teddy he would have to stay with them, and to go wherever they went. So when Teddy got to the fair, he went wherever his parents went.

But soon he got bored, because his parents were not going to any games. So Teddy decided to take five tickets and go on a Merry-go-round. So he took his tickets and went to the Merry-go-round. After five rides, Teddy thought he would go back to his parents. But when he came for them, they weren't there.

Poor Teddy was lost, because he didn't listen. He walked a little, and decided to ask where the information center was, so he could tell them he was lost. He asked a man, and the man showed Teddy where it was. Teddy told his name, and every other thing they wanted. So they asked for Teddy's parents, and they came and picked up Teddy. They told Teddy that he didn't listen. From that day on Teddy always listened.

by Lisa

Intermediate level children can also study type-three conflict and subsequently write stories embodying it. After such study, fifth and sixth grade children recently composed these stories. The first two are about main characters who are selfish and, thus, indifferent to the needs of others.

One day Susie Flutsnot was walking to school. On her way she ran into a farmer who had caught his sleeve in a plow.

"Oh, help me, Susie. Please help me," he cried.

"If you were a good farmer, you would not have gotten yourself caught," Susie answered as she continued to school.

Then she heard a voice say, "I am stuck in the mud. Please help me." It was a cow.

"A heavy animal like you should know not to walk in the mud," she said, and she continued to school.

As she approached the school, she slipped and fell down. Then the farmer walked by.

"Oh, help me farmer. Take my homework to the teacher," she cried.

"An intelligent person would not have fallen down," said the farmer as he walked by.

Then the cow walked by.

"Please help me. The farmer would not," she pleaded.

"I don't blame the farmer—you would not help him. And you did not help me when I was in the mud," said the cow, as she walked away.

And so Susie Flutsnot didn't get her homework to school, and was expelled.

by Jody

Once there was a little boy who lived in a little village, and he had a little mom, a little dad, and a little dog. But the little boy was very mean and selfish.

One day he was playing at school, and it was time for school to begin. The bell had no one to ring it. So the bell said to the little boy, "Little boy, please ring me." But the little boy said, "No! Ring yourself," and he went on playing.

One day a big giant came to the little village for breakfast. He saw the little boy playing in the school yard. The giant picked the little boy up, and opened his big mouth to eat him up! Just then the little boy cried, "Help me, Bell. Ring yourself so the people of the village can help me." But the bell said, "No. You would not ring me, so why should I ring now?" So the giant ate the little boy. So don't be mean and selfish, or you might end up like the little boy.

by Cory

The following story, exploring the consequences of an inflammatory temper, is written rather remarkably in first person.

"Oh, my God, I can't believe it! I really killed her. My wife, the one I've loved and cherished for 47 years.

It was Friday, December 11, 1971. My wife and I were eating supper when she brought up ages. We were kidding each other, saying big and small numbers. Then she said to me, 'Charles, now that I'm 69, you must be 74.'

'I never in my life dreamed she even knew my age, or how much older I was. So I said, 'Are you kidding? I'm 69, too.'

'Don't be silly, Charles. I know as well as you do that you're 74,' she said. I couldn't stand it any longer, my ears were ringing. I took our butcher knife and slit her throat. I was glad I ended her life, but now it seems I ended mine too.

I can't stand it. My eyes are bloodshot, I stagger when I walk; but worst of all, I'm afraid to go near anything! Every time I think, 'It was her fault! Why should I get the blame?' I think of five reasons to tell the police. I wish I was dead. I can't live!

Finally I got enough courage to go out of the house. I got out my car and drove to the police station. When I got there my mind went crazy. I cried out, 'I did it! I did it! I KILLED HER!'

After an hour they finally calmed me down. At least it's all over, and my mind is at ease.

by Wendy

OTHER LITERATURE-BASED CONFLICT POSSIBILITIES

A lyric story illustrated lavishly by Ezra Jack Keats has been of use in helping children understand the first type of conflict, person versus person.[26] It should be fairly easy for children to analyze what caused the conflict, what motivated the poor man to work toward the resolution, and how the king and the poor man had to change before the conflict could be resolved. Discussion following the reading of the story might focus on such questions as:

- Why did the king want to build the fountain?
- Who was aware of the problem?
- What kept him from solving the problem?
- What was it in what the poor man said that changed the king's mind?

After discussion of the story, which would help children understand the nature of conflict, assign a writing problem for them to solve. For example, suppose that the principal of the school has decided to change their outside play area into a parking lot as a convenience for visitors. One day, a child overhears two teachers discussing this possibility. Have children write, dictate, or draw a story about how the child could help solve the problem.

An example of the second kind of conflict, the individual versus fate or a force larger than the individual, is employed in a story about Uncle Vanya.[27] The special power he has wins recognition and fame for Uncle Vanya. Before long the magic causes a special problem for the villagers, who fear the sunflower may prevent the sun from reaching them. On their own the villagers are unable to destroy the sunflower, so they insist that Vanya do something. The story is especially helpful in having children consider if a special power can sometimes be helpful and sometimes not. After a discussion of Uncle Vanya's power—a mixed blessing at

26 Lloyd Alexander, *The King's Fountain.*
27 Shan Ellentuck, *A Sunflower as Big as the Sun.*

best—have the children think of other powers people might have. Then let them make up a story of a person who has that power, describing how it was used and how it created a conflict.

EVALUATION OF PLOT

As in evaluation of characterization and setting, the ability to evaluate plot develops slowly over an extended period of time. Because teachers are interested in having children evaluate the effectiveness of their own writing, they should ask the children questions to cause them to think analytically about what they have written.

In regard to plot, the beginning questions will usually deal with some aspect of sequence:

- Can we follow along with what is happening in the story? Are there some places we are confused about what is happening?
- Are there some places where things don't happen in the order they should? Is there some reason why something is told about out of order?

You may also want to ask questions about the interest level of the plot:

- Are the ideas in my stories becoming more interesting? Does something exciting happen to the main character?
- Is there some place in my story where something else needs to happen? Or, is there some place in my story where there is too much happening?

Later, with older children who have had some experience in evaluating their own writing, you may want to ask questions about plot direction or about treatment of plot:

- Am I learning how to make plots go in more than one direction? Can I sometimes start at the end of my story and work backwards, or in the middle and go in both directions, instead of always having to start at the beginning and work toward the end?
- Am I learning how to write different kinds of plots, including both realistic and fantasy ones?

It is important that children have opportunities to confront such questions. With young children such evaluation sessions will usually be in a group context as children reflect on a group story they have composed. With older children evaluation sessions usually occur individually, during a conference time the teacher provides in which the child is asked to look analytically at what he or she has written and make judgments about it. Such analysis is important if children are to develop the editing ability mentioned in chapter one and explained further in chapter eight.

6

USING
FIGURATIVE
LANGUAGE

The river is a piece of sky—or so it seems to one writer.[1] Another tells us that the sun is a golden earring.[2] In both cases the author's use of figurative language gives us a unique view and captures an unusual way of thinking about a commonplace object. Therein lies the power of figurative language and the justification for devoting attention to it in a writing program. For it is by the purposeful use of figures of speech that writers arrest their readers' attention, causing them to ponder a particular perception and way of telling about it. In this writing program children are introduced consciously to figurative language and challenged to express themselves in these ways for the richness such expression gives to writing.

KINDS OF FIGURATIVE LANGUAGE

The total array of figures of speech available to writers of English is wide. One writer has identified thirteen such

[1] John Ciardi, "The River is a Piece of Sky," in *The Sound of Poetry*, ed. Mary C. Austin and Queenie B. Mills, p. 200.
[2] Natalie Belting, *The Sun Is a Golden Earring*.

figures that are used in literature for children and that they should thus understand.[3] These run the gamut from simple forms like similes to such arcane forms as trope [4] and metonymy.[5] In the elementary school writing program we will be concerned primarily with simile and metaphor as the forms most within the writing capabilities of young children.

The simile, which is simpler, should be introduced first. This type of comparison uses the words *like* or *as,* and leads the reader to see the resemblance of one object to another because of its readily apparent structure. The metaphor, by contrast, is a statement that one object being compared *is* the other, without the use of the signal words *like* or *as.* The two examples in the first paragraph are, thus, metaphors. The metaphor is a more sophisticated comparison, more difficult to understand, and it should be introduced later in the writing program.

LITERATURE INPUT

As in other strands in this program, literature plays a crucial role in introducing children to a concept. The samples of literature that the teacher reads can help children understand the idea being considered. There are many sources of similes to share with children, among them several elementary language series that introduce the idea.[6]

[3] Emerald V. Dechant, *Improving the Teaching of Reading,* pp. 389–92.

[4] Tropes are words created for a specific occasion or use but not adapted into the general language. Many of these are included in *Alice in Wonderland.* "Twas brillig and the slithy toves . . ." is an example.

[5] Metonymy is the use of one object for another to which it is related. Examples include using "counting heads" for "counting people" and "ship of state" for "government."

[6] See, for example, Muriel Crosby, ed., *The World of Language,* bk. 3, p. 100, or bk. 5, pp. 345–46. Material on figurative language is included in each level of this series, which presents the most complete consideration of this topic available in any elementary series. You might also consult examples

We also find similes used in picture books for the youngest children. Often these deal with animal images. One author provides a vivid picture: "Like a mother hen, I would wish to have my children and see them play around me."[7] Comparing children to animals is often done, sometimes irreverently. Gaeddert describes Nancy who "hopped down the hall like a kangaroo."[8] Cohen describes Dan who puts his tongue in his lip and his fingers in his ear so he can look "just like a monkey."[9] Coatsworth includes images of a goat "as white as the foam of the sea," who lives under palm trees that make noises "as though they were whispering together."[10]

We often find similes in poetry as well as in picture books. You might share Rachel Field's "Taxis"[11] with young children so they can enjoy the comparison made between the taxis and spools of colored thread rolling along the avenues. Contrast this description of automobiles with the one by Tresselt,[12] in which the cars—almost buried in snow—are compared with big, fat raisins.

Many other examples of poetic simile are included in a book by Merriam.[13] The poet talks about vowels in words that open "wide as waves in the moon-blue sea." A more extended comparison is included in "Simile: Willow and

in *Elementary School English*, bk. 3, pp. 172–73, and bk. 5, pp. 126–30. Or see H. Thompson Fillmer et al., *Patterns of Language*, bk. 6, pp. 114–16, 121, 150. Another treatment of the topic is included in Cornelia Nachbar et al., *Flying Free*, Vol. 6, pp. 6–8, 318.

[7] Kazue Mizumura, *If I Were a Mother.*

[8] Lou Ann Gaeddert, *Noisy Nancy Norris.*

[9] Miriam Cohen, *Will I Have a Friend?* Charming muted-pastel illustrations by Lillian Hoban enhance this story dealing realistically with a kindergarten child's concern the first day of school.

[10] Elizabeth Coatsworth, *Lonely Maria.*

[11] Included in Grace Huffard, Carlisle, and Ferris, eds., *My Poetry Book.* A wide-ranging collection of poems grouped according to topics, the book features rather dated, though interesting, illustrations by Willy Pogany.

[12] Alvin Tresselt, *White Snow, Bright Snow.* The book features broadly done three-color illustrations by Roger Duvoisin.

[13] Eve Merriam, *It Doesn't Always Have to Rhyme*, pp. 3, 27.

Ginkgo," designed for older children. Ms. Merriam compares the willow to the fine lines of an etching, and the ginkgo to a crude sketch. Each of the five stanzas offers comparisons. Another poem, "Cliché," is useful in helping children examine the originality of their own simile writing. In it the poet asks many questions to encourage originality of expression. For example: Is toast really the warmest thing you can think of?

Equally helpful is a recent book, the title of which is a simile, *Green Is Like a Meadow of Grass*.[14] In it the selector has collected both similes and metaphors written by children. These children wrote poetry about pine trees that are like giant hair brushes, with pine cones like snarls to be brushed out. Other nature images included the sound of raindrops on flowers, likened to the sound of ladybugs walking on grass. Insightful metaphors abound, written by even the youngest children. One poem describes trees and bushes wearing nightgowns of snow, another tells of daffodils that are pieces of sun fallen to the earth, yet another of a seashell with a shiny clean scrubbed face.

Another possibility is the collection of poems in *This Way, Delight*.[15] In one the poet tells us of a boy sitting "as still as a stone." Or consider using "A Birthday," which contains many similes.

A delightful collection of poems that make use of figurative language is one by Cole.[16] The poet describes a strange collection of children: one whose voice "was as hoarse as a crow," another who was "like a little bit of thread," another who was "red as any rosebud or geranium," while yet another was as "deaf as the buoy out at the Nore."

Also useful are poems from a book edited by the distinguished black poet Arnold Adoff; many are rich in simile

---

14 Nancy Larrick, ed., *Green Is Like a Meadow of Grass*.
15 Herbert Read, *This Way, Delight*, pp. 9, 46.
16 William Cole, ed., *Beastly Boys and Ghastly Girls*.

imagery.[17] "Color," "Blackberry Street," or "The Truth is Quite Messy," would be helpful in studying similes.

OTHER POETRY POSSIBILITIES

Almost any collection of poetry will provide many examples of similes to be shared with children, both for the enjoyment they bring and also for the further understanding of the form that they develop. Among those you might use are:

The Malibu and Other Poems by Myra Livingston Cohn.
  The beautifully etched, small line drawings in black and white deserve as much careful contemplation as do the poems. Use "Here I Am," in which the poet paints the eternally renewed conflict between bully and oppressed; the bully is described as having "big red fists and fat cheeks, and mouth like a bursted balloon" (p. 36).

Words Words Words by Mary O'Neill.
  Share "Feelings About Words," in which the poet talks about words that clink like ice in a drink. Or use "Patience or Concomdure?," which uses many extended comparisons:

> For patience sounds
> Like a lady in brown
> Ironing pleats in her forehead
> To further her frown.
>
> [p. 52]

A Snail's a Failure Socially by Kaye Starbird.
  In one of the poems she describes the fate of Whistling Willie, the proprietor of the dingy neighbor-

[17] Arnold Adoff, ed., *Black Out Loud.*

hood market, who was "small and round with hair like a dried-out thistle" (p. 16).

A Child's Calendar by John Updike.

The book is enhanced with Nancy Burkert's serene illustrations; this time they are done in limited color but with much attention to fine details. In describing March, the poet uses similes:

> Pale crocuses
> Poke through the ground
> Like noses come
> To sniff around.

PROSE AS A SOURCE

Prose for children of any age offers a wide variety of similes for enjoyment and study. A perennial favorite uses many similes in the main characters, penguins. The size of the penguin is about the same as a small child, though it "looked more like a little gentleman." Its flippers, black on the outside and white inside, looked "like the sleeve of a tailcoat." It was difficult to tell the two penguins apart, for they were "as alike as two peas." [18]

The work of Elizabeth Enright bears some similarities to the book by the Atwaters. In each a very particular sense of time and place is created. In addition, Enright creates very funny stories, which children enjoy. Much of her writing is useful in studying figurative language. Some of the similes she writes are quite simple. In talking about a county fair, she writes of little pigs "as white as thistledown." In the

[18] Richard Atwater and Florence Atwater, *Mr. Popper's Penguins*, pp. 18, 21, 68. The whimsical black and white illustrations by Robert Lawson add considerably to the charm of the book.

same book she describes the heat, so intense it seemed "like being inside of a drum." A snake moved "like a drawn ribbon through the wet ferns." Children may need help understanding her description of a threshing machine: "Straw and chaff flew out of a pipe that looked like a dinosaur's neck." [19] At other times the similes she writes are more complex: ". . . and the thing that made many of the trees seem spooky was the fact that they were draped and festooned with matted honeysuckle vines, so that they looked less like trees than like great shawled figures. . . ." [20]

A modern fantasy that children enjoy describes, instead of animals, miniature people. As Homily, the mother, is reprimanding her daughter Arrietty for slinging an onion ring around her shoulder while wearing her clean jersey, she asks: "Do you want to smell like a bit-bucket?" Pod, the father, is caught "like a bird" halfway up the curtain by the dreaded "human beans," whom the family feared.[21]

Much of the delightful humor found in a recent book by Konigsburg is due to the similes the author has created. Elizabeth describes her Thanksgiving costume with scorn: "I looked like a Pilgrim who had made a bad trade with the Indians." Jennifer's costume, on the contrary, intrigued her, partly because of its smell: "She smelled a little bit like mothballs, but I happen to especially like that smell in Autumn." An aural image is created when Elizabeth discovers, in her Saturday meetings at the library with Jennifer, that Jennifer whispers "beautifully, with many nice sssssssssssounds, coming out like steam out of a kettle."[22]

Similes dealing with sounds are common; for example:

[19] Elizabeth Enright, *Thimble Summer*, pp. 3, 28, 66, 103.

[20] Elizabeth Enright, *Gone Away Lake*, pp. 169, 175. Children would also enjoy *Then There Were Five* or *The Saturdays*.

[21] Mary Norton, *The Borrowers*, pp. 23, 31.

[22] E. L. Konigsburg, *Jennifer, Hecate, Macbeth, William McKinley, and Me, Elizabeth*, p. 25.

". . . the sound of his teacher's voice—dotted with 'i's,' and crossed with 't's,' and sprinkled with commas and semicolons." [23]

Suggestions for how to make children more aware of similes by using historical fiction are included in the Nebraska Curriculum treatment of a story for younger children, *Caroline and Her Kettle Named Maud*.[24] Further help with similes is provided in the unit based on a story by Wilder.[25]

Realistic fiction also contains excellent examples of similes to share with children. Keith Robertson has described a perennial problem for children. Henry, in talking about Aunt Mable trying to find friends for him comments: ". . . the last thing I wanted was for her to go scouting around to find boys for me to play with. When grownups do that they always pick someone who is about as interesting as a plate of cold spaghetti. . . ." This is a truly unforgettable image, as is the one of Uncle Al, who is nonplussed by Henry's energy when they carry suitcases upstairs: "He's half my size, yet he hasn't turned a hair, and I'm puffing like a steam engine." [26]

Sounder is another book of realistic fiction that contains many memorable scenes, made that way in part by the similes used. In describing the dry dust under the cabin, Armstrong tells us that it tasted "like lime and grease." He

[23] Felice Holman, *The Cricket Winter*. The improbable story of Simms, a boy whose inventive talents are ignored by his parents. How Simms meets Cricket and his encounter with the other inhabitants under the house makes for engrossing reading.

[24] Miriam E. Mason, *Caroline and Her Kettle Named Maud*. The story contains many similes. It is used as a core text, and several language-exploration suggestions are included in *A Curriculum for English*. The series of graded curriculum guides is a commendable attempt to build a multi-faceted language-arts program around literature.

[25] Laura Ingalls Wilder, "The Little House on the Prairie," in *A Curriculum for English*, bk. 4, pp. 89–100. Considerable attention is given to the similes written by the author and to using them as a base for writing by children.

[26] Keith Robertson, *Henry Reed, Inc.*, pp. 13, 20.

provides a memorable olfactory image in writing that the dust smelled stale and dead, like old carcasses and snakes. When his mother told the boy a Bible story, she described the water that "moved in little ripples like curtains in a breeze." [27]

In contrast with the above fiction, we might share *Onion John* with children, for it is also rich in similes, though the location, characters, and problem are very different than in *Sounder*. The author describes the procedure for making a fire; using a thin round stick and a small bow, "you work the bow back and forth like you were playing a bull fiddle." A vital visual image is included in the picture of the cellar, "where it was black except for a square red glow, like a stage, lighted up by the open furnace door." [28]

In another popular book for older children, Clark has written this comparison: "The boy's thoughts were whirling like the foaming rapids on the far side of the valley." [29]

A memorable book for older children contains several examples of similes. In developing the adventures of Jesse, Fox describes one of his shipmates: "Curry sang a tune to himself in a horrible cracked voice that sounded as if it had been fried in lard." In describing how he felt during a bout of seasickness, Jesse says, "I felt that if I didn't keep my mouth tightly closed, I should be turned inside out like a garment that was to be laundered." And finally, in describing one of the most despised crew members, Jesse says, "His mouth remained open like a small dark cave where nothing lives." [30]

These are but a few of many books that can be used as literature input when the teacher prepares children for conscious study and writing of similes.

[27] William Armstrong, *Sounder*, pp. 40, 42.
[28] Joseph Krumgold, *Onion John*, pp. 69, 75.
[29] Ann Nolan Clark, *Secret of the Andes*, p. 14.
[30] Paula Fox, *The Slave Dancer*, pp. 52, 85, 137.

SIMILES IN THE WRITING PROGRAM

The introduction of figurative language begins with the very youngest children. Kindergarten teachers should search for writing that includes similes and in sharing this writing, point out the similes, identifying them simply as interesting ways to say something. An appropriate comment might be, "Doesn't the way the author said that make a good picture for us to see!" No attempt should be made at this stage to introduce the term or explain it. Impressional treatment, described earlier, is the goal. Some children will notice, others may remember; simple enjoyment is enough at this stage.

With older children, perhaps second or no later than third grade, we consciously plan to introduce the concept. Teachers should share many samples of writing, drawing from children the definition of *simile,* which evolves as they sense the similarity in the examples. Then the term may be introduced, not as a word to be tested cognitively, but rather as a concept to expand children's awareness of language and what it can do.

Later, children should be asked to write similes. At first, this is done simply as an experience in organizing thought and making comparisons. No attempt should be made at the beginning to incorporate such comparisons or descriptions into stories or poems.

One successful way to begin is by using an audio-visual approach. We have had singular success by using the book, *A Picture Has a Special Look.*[31] Originally intended to sensitize children to a variety of art media and their distinctive characteristics, this is written using many similes. The

[31] Helen Borten, *A Picture Has a Special Look.* It is also available in a filmstrip and record combination from Weston Woods Studios (LTR-054). I usually use the audio-visual format for class motivation and have the book available for children to enjoy later if they wish.

filmstrip-record combination, which accompanies the book, is used as motivation, followed by a discussion of the author's similes. After the discussion, we make a list of the "simile stems" used by the author. These include:

- as bold as . . .
- as frightened as . . .
- as gradual as . . .
- like a . . .

After identifying the simile stems, we ask children to suggest other stems. Then children write completions for them.

Some third grade children recently created the following similes after this introduction motivation:

- as simple as an egg
- as tight as shrunk pants
- as thin as a stamp
- as mean as a horse that kicks
- as small as plankton
- as tall as a giraffe on stilts
- as stupid as a potato
- as lovable as my relatives

Another third grade group contributed these:

- as frail as a very thin wine glass
- as simple as scribbling
- as lumpy as a gourd
- as bold as chocolate pudding in a white bowl
- as old as a white dandelion.

You'll notice that the above are not, technically, complete similes. We don't know, for example, *what* was "as tight as shrunk pants." The teacher should not insist upon complete similes during the first writing experience. Acquainting children with the idea and getting them to complete one side of the simile stem is very satisfactory work for an initial writing experience. Later, we might use a record about similes, to remotivate children for another simile writing experience.[32]

At some time during the unit on similes, the teacher will want to give some consideration to trite similes, developing the idea that the most effective similes are ones that help us see an unusual comparison or visual picture. Almost anyone can write, "as busy as a bee." It takes a more unusual command of language to write, as one perceptive fifth grader did recently: "as busy as an electric typewriter."

In the initial stages, simile writing may often lack originality:

- as sticky as molasses
- as fluffy as a cloud
- as tall as a giraffe
- as slow as a turtle
- as soft as cotton

Teachers should accept these at the beginning, knowing that children are trying to make comparisons. But it is important not to be satisfied with such conventionalized comparisons, for it is the unusual comparison we are seeking. By the kind of questions they ask, teachers encourage children to reflect upon experience, to test new comparisons, to search for language they have not used previously. For instance, if a child wrote the simile "as sticky as molasses," the teacher might use the following questions:

[32] An effective motivation for intermediate grade children is "Similes," in the record set *Developing Language Arts Skills*, available from The Society for Visual Education, Chicago, Ill. Also of use is "Metaphors and Similes—Imagery!" in the record and filmstrip set, *What Is Poetry?*, no. 9, available from Caedmon Records (CFS-501).

- What else is sticky?
- What is sticky that doesn't look it?
- Are different things sticky at different times? For example?

Through careful work like this, the teacher can lead children to more unusual expression of thought in similes. In addition, the teacher works to help children develop the ability to write the complete simile, an ability even young children can develop. Some kindergarten children recently dictated these similes to their teacher:

- My fingers move as fast as rain.
- My toes move as wiggly as a worm.
- My eyes are as green as the leaves on a flower.
- A rainbow is curved with color like paint.

The ability to write similes is one thing; the ability to incorporate them into stories is a more sophisticated skill. Initial writing experiences concentrate on the ability to write similes. When a teacher senses the children are ready, the emphasis should be changed to incorporating similes into stories.

A kindergarten teacher had worked with her children on similes and she felt they were ready to try using their ability in the context of a story. She shared *Swimmy* with them (see reference, chapter five, p. 126). Following this experience, she asked them to write an adventure for Swimmy, using similes. Her children dictated the following stories:

Swimmy's Adventure

It was exciting. It was fun. Swimmy went down
in the sea. He played with a whale like a summer
breeze plays with a flower.

by Stephen

Swimmy lived in the time of the dinosaurs. There

was a giant killer squid in the sea. His nose was as sharp as an arrow, and his tentacles moved as fast as a whip. Swimmy looked as little as a sea shell, and he darted like lightening. So the squid didn't see him coming. Swimmy bit the squid in the heart and he went diving down like a submarine and he died.

by Bobby

Two of the boys in the class chose to change the time and locale to link the stories they wrote to war.

Swimmy was helping the Army. He bit a hole in an aircraft boat and it went down like a can filling with water.

by John

Flash! The Japanese are bombing Pearl Harbor. Swimmy joins the Navy. He is brave as a lion and his fins are as powerful as a submarine. He helps by pushing the torpedos back at the Japanese.

by Eddie

In reading the above stories it is possible to react that the similes are too concentrated, that the writing seems artificial because of the number of similes included in a brief story. However, it is important to keep in mind that this was an initial attempt. When children are asked to use similes in stories, they often overuse the device at first. As a beginning attempt to incorporate similes into the context of a story, these are impressive. Later in the writing program the teacher can expect that children will become more selective in the similes they include in the stories. Another example at a different grade level will show how older children respond to this idea.

A third grade teacher, interested in having children incorporate similes into stories they wrote, set up a writing problem based on *Swimmy*. She read the story to the children. They were to create another adventure for him but, in addition, were to incorporate similes into their writing. Stories written by the children included these:

> One day Swimmy saw a school of fish as big as two blackboards put together. He asked them what school they went to, and they said, "Get out! Can't you see we're in school?" They laughed so much that China shook! They laughed as long as it took Apollo Twelve to go to the moon.
>
> Soon Swimmy saw a whale as tall as two schools put together. Swimmy was so scared that he broke the ice. The ice was as thick as a MacDonald's quarter pounder. Swimmy was as slow as a trutle. The whale was as fast as a sattelite. A fisherman killed the whale just in time for Swimmy to escape. He was as happy as Skylab Three to get home.
>
> by Paul

> One day Swimmy turned blue as the sea. A leaf fell down on the sea. It was as fragile as a snowflake. Swimmy got on. It broke. A boy threw a stick at him. The stick was as hard as an octopus's grip, and as long as a fishing rod.
>
> Swimmy turned red. The doctor got there. Swimmy said, "I thought you were as fast as a rocket?" "Not any more," said the doctor. "Now I'm as slow as a leaf that is falling from a tree." "Hurry up, I want to be as black as tar again." So the doctor gave him a pill, and he turned yellow, red, purple, and finally black as tar again.
>
> by Jeff

The same teacher provided a different story motivation
but with the same problem: incorporating similes into composition. She read *Giant John* (See chapter three, page 85)
and again asked her children to write an adventure for the
main character, using similes. Among those written by the
children were these:

Once upon a time there was a boy named Giant
John. He was as tall as a skyscraper. One day
Giant John was walking through the woods to get
some wood. He had his ax. It was as sharp as a
paper cut. He cut three trees at one time. Then he
brought the wood home.

Years went by. By now Giant John was as tall
as the moon and as old as a Grandmother. He
grew a beard as fuzzy as sheep. He was then as
playful as a kitten.

It started to rain. The clouds were as gray as hair
when you are old. Giant John was as lucky as
finding a four leaf clover, because he needed a
shower.

One day Giant John was asked to be in the circus. He went. He was the man who lifted weights.
He was in the circus for the rest of his life.

by Monica

One day Giant John was very lonely. He wanted
someone to play with as much as you would want
to have fun. But there was no one his size. He was
as big as a full grown oak tree. He said to himself,
"I'll go out and take a walk in the meadow. It's
as green as a forest of trees with leaves on them.
I'll think as hard as a rock about how to find a
friend."

He got back to his house, which was as tall as

the Empire State Building, and as wide as if you lay it down. Then he thought, "I'll listen to the radio. I'll feel better than a person at their own birthday party." So he turned the radio on louder than an avalanche of boulders. But it made his ear drums hurt as bad as ever.

But after that he had a great idea. "There are more people than could fit in a station, listening to the radio these days." He went as far as a bullet down to the radio station. He asked as quick as a road runner runs, "Can I make an announcement?" The announcer said, "If it's a quick one." Giant John said it would be. He said, "Any lonely giant can come to Giant John's at the edge of the forest." He waited. No one came. A couple of days later he felt as bad as a person would if his mom forgot his birthday.

Then someone knocked on the door. He went as fast as Superman to the door. It was a boy. He said, "I heard an ad on the radio and tried to find your house, but had bad luck. Well, my name is Giant Joe and I am very lonely." "Well," said Giant John, "I guess you will be my best friend."

by Kathy

WRITING METAPHOR

Another form children can be taught to write is the metaphor, although this is more difficult because the comparison is not directly stated. The idea should probably not be introduced consciously before the later intermediate grades, though initial impressional sharing of metaphor can begin before then.

There are, as with similes, many sources of metaphors to share with children. As in other strands of the program, much literature input is required before writing of metaphor can be begun. Several language series books provide useful material.[33]

Most poetry anthologies contain many samples to use with children.[34] One poet used metaphor in creating a memorable visual picture of a train:

A Modern Dragon
A train is a dragon that roars through the dark.
He wriggles his tail as he sends up a spark.
He pierces the night with his one yellow eye.
And all the earth trembles when he rushes by.[35]

In addition to poetry anthologies, books by individual poets include much helpful material.[36] You might begin with the charming poem, "Metaphor," in which the poet tells us that a poem is a cloud, a tree, a city, a sea, and a golden mystery.[37] Read the poem to children several different times on different days; this allows the rhythm, word choices, and imagery to become part of the children's consciousness. Then explore with them the metaphors the poet has created. You might use such questions as:

- In what ways does the poet say a poem is a cloud? Why is this the case?

[33] Some elementary language series attempt to help children with this idea. See, for example, Andrew Schiller et al., *Language and How to Use It,* bk. 6, pp. 156–58. Or see H. Thompson Fillmer et al., *Patterns of Language,* bk. 6, pp. 116–17, 121, 150. Another treatment of the topic is included in Cornelia Nachbar et al., *Flying Free,* Vol. 6., p. 6.

[34] See, for example, May Hill Arbuthnot, *The Arbuthnot Anthology.*

[35] Rowena Bennett, "A Modern Dragon," in *The Sound of Poetry,* ed. Mary C. Austin and Queenie B. Mills, p. 160. In this useful collection the introductory material on reasons for using poetry with children and how to choose appropriate poetry is very helpful.

[36] Aileen Fisher, *Cricket in a Thicket.* With easily identifiable black and white lithographs by Feodor Rojankovsky, this small volume contains many examples of figurative language. When studying metaphor, use "Pine Music," in which the poet talks of the harp in the pines, a house of green, unseen except for the wind who strums the strings for the listening rabbits.

[37] Merriam, *It Doesn't Always Have to Rhyme,* p. 27.

- Are there other ways a poem is cloudlike?
- In what ways is a poem a tree? What kind of a tree does a poem seem like to you?
- In what ways is a poem citylike? What kind and size of city do you think the poet had in mind?
- What is a sea like? What are the qualities of seas that are memorable? How is a poem a sea?

One editor has presented extensive evidence that children express themselves quite naturally in metaphor.[38] The book demonstrates effectively to children that they can become adept metaphor writers. Over the course of a month, the entire book could be shared with your group of children to provide literature input leading to the writing of metaphor.

Prose also provides a rich source of metaphor to be shared with children. Metaphor has appealed to writers of children's literature for a long time. The work of Enright is full of such delightful examples as: "A large herd of furniture grazed on a red carpet. . . ."[39]

Fox, mentioned earlier in connection with the similes in her Newbery Award winning book, is also a beautiful metaphor writer. For example, she has Jesse, whose father is dead, comment on the lack of male influence in his life: ". . . I wouldn't count the parson, who was a stick notched with pious sayings."[40]

UNDERSTANDING FIGURATIVE LANGUAGE

As some of the examples used here may have indicated, figurative language sometimes presents problems to children in that the meaning involved is not always readily apparent.

[38] Larrick, *Green is Like a Meadow of Grass.*
[39] Enright, *Gone Away Lake,* p. 38.
[40] Fox, p. 47.

When Mary Norton speaks of the danger of smelling like a bit-bucket, the meaning may need to be explained to children. Similarly, the metaphor by Fox included above illustrates the inherent problem of figurative language: potential lack of understanding of the meaning intended by the author. As adults we may indeed easily understand Fox's figure; nevertheless we must guard against assuming that children will also understand it without help. Just what *does* Fox mean when she has Jesse call the parson a stick? What ideas is she attempting to convey to the reader? What would be the best way to help children understand this metaphor?

One reason for planning a unit on figurative language is that children encounter many examples of such language, both in reading books and in trade books. Robertson [41] presents evidence about the frquency with which authors make use of such figures. She further suggests that if teachers expect children to understand and appreciate what the author has written, specific study of such language may be necessary. To plan such a study of figurative language, the teacher must be able to look analytically at literature and consider two things:

- There may be vocabulary involved that is familiar to us but unfamiliar to children. When Cole speaks of a character being "deaf as a buoy," we must be sure children know what the word means.
- The simile may make use of a comparison that was easily understandable at one time but may now be confusing to children. For example, when Enright describes a boy with a few teeth missing,

[41] Jean E. Robertson, "Figurative Language," in *Instructor*, November 1973, pp. 50–51. The article is helpful primarily because it cites some unpublished research dealing with the extent of figures used by authors and with children's understanding of the figures.

she writes: "When you smile, it looks just like the front of a Buick." [42] This communicates meaning to those of us who grew up when that automobile's grill featured closely spaced vertical bars, but, without help, it won't communicate meaning to today's children.

A pair of authors, with a similar concern to Robertson's, have devised a test to determine the level of understanding children have of figures of speech.[43] You might find it helpful to use the test with your children before starting a unit on figures of speech. Finally, other suggestions about how to work with metaphor are included in an article by this author.[44] In closing, it would be difficult to find a better way to summarize this concern over understanding of figurative speech than with the cartoon below.

© 1973 United Features Syndicate, Inc.

[42] Enright, *Gone Away Lake.*

[43] Jean M. Anderson and Martha Kahler, "It's Raining Cats and Dogs," *Instructor,* January 1971, pp. 69–70. The article is useful because of the list of fifteen suggestions for classroom activities to promote understanding of figures of speech, and because of the bibliography included.

[44] John Warren Stewig, "Metaphor and Children's Writing," *Elementary English,* February 1966, pp. 121–23.

7

POETRY:
SOLUTIONS
TO A PROBLEM

The Wind
The wind shall roar,
Roar whispers in your ear,
The wind shall soar,
Soar through the sky,
The wind shall sing,
Sing with me,
The wind shall run,
Run with the sea . . . free, free.

by Julie

Young children react eagerly to rhyme, saying with delight the repeated lines of Mother Goose, singing enthusiastically the poetry in songs they are taught, and responding sensitively to the rhythmic pulse of poems read by their teachers. Most young children seem to have a natural appetite for poetry.

Yet in talking with older children and their teachers, we too often find a very different response than was present a few years before. Children respond less enthusiastically, and teachers report difficulty in finding poems children will like.

Two researchers recently asked children to write a story, an expository paragraph, and a poem. Can you guess to which of these the children responded negatively? The groans were reserved for the poetry writing, while children responded willingly to writing an expository paragraph and a story.

Why the negative reactions to poetry, too commonly found among upper elementary children? The question is especially perplexing considering the gusto of children's appetite for poetry, nursery rhymes, and verse when they come to school. What happens to dull children's appreciation for poetry written by others and to make them apprehensive about writing it themselves?

To answer these questions, we need to examine some misconceptions about poetry that are held by many children. Looking at the misconceptions may help us identify possible causes of children's attitudes about poetry and possible means of changing these attitudes. In doing this we will spend much time considering which poetry to share with children and how to share it. This is not to avoid the problem of how to motivate children to write poetry, since the focus of this book is improving children's composition skills. Rather, this emphasis on poetry input is to establish a basic idea: In order to write poetry effectively, children need to hear great quantities of poetry read effectively.

MISCONCEPTIONS ABOUT POETRY

Children are in fact "exposed" to poetry throughout the elementary schools, but such exposure frequently and inadvertently develops three misconceptions detrimental to children's appreciation.

Misconception One

Poetry is rhymed. This is undoubtedly the most universal misconception children have about poetry. Ask any group of randomly selected children to define poetry, and rhyme will figure in most definitions. The antidote for this, to be discussed later, is to share many types of unrhymed poetry with children at all grade levels. New collections including a wide diversity of poems make this easy to do now.[1]

Misconception Two

Poetry is pretty. For too many children this equation limits their interest in poetry. Too often children think of poetry in terms of delicate images of beautiful, often fragile things, encompassed in a sun-lit world where little action takes place. The teacher has an obligation to choose poetry that deals in honest ways with a wide variety of topics, some of which may not seem, at first consideration, to be suitable for children. Older children should hear "Richard Corey," [2] for example, simply because it deals with a topic considered taboo in schools.

Misconception Three

Nothing much happens in poetry. We have fortunately moved beyond such lyric, visually memorable but essentially

[1] See Stephen Dunning et al., eds., *Reflections on a Gift of Watermelon Pickle.* . . . Illustrated with dramatic, evocative black and white photographs, the collection of poems includes many different unrhymed forms. Or see Dunning et al., eds., *Some Haystacks Don't Even Have Any Needle.* Full-color reproductions of contemporary paintings complement the contemporary poems.

[2] Edwin A. Robinson, "Richard Corey," in Louis Untermeyer, ed., *Modern American Poetry,* p. 123. Useful with older children, the poem is effective because of the shock of the last line, which destroys dramatically the image created until then. You might use the Simon and Garfunkle recording of the poem, included in *Sounds of Silence,* Columbia (CS 9269).

static images as presented in the "host of golden daffodils" we adults knew as children. Children today are still too often treated to static, descriptive poetry in which little conflict and resolution occur. Recently observing in a kindergarten, I heard to my dismay that a dreadful ditty that likens pussywillows to a kitty with a silver gray coat is still being read to children. It is a poem in which absolutely nothing happens.

A corollary of the last two misconceptions is the idea, unfortunately too pervasive among intermediate grade boys, that poetry is essentially for girls. Often unwitting teachers, presenting a sequence of poems about "pretty" topics, described in detail, lose the interest of both boys and girls. Children need to be exposed to the direct fresh work of David McCord,[3] James Reeves,[4] and Harry Behn,[5] for the alternatives they present to much of the poetry now in anthologies for children.

CHANGING THE IMAGE

What can be done to change children's misconceptions about poetry? Since most children receive whatever exposure they have to poetry in school, it is the teacher's job to examine both what poetry is being shared with children and the nature of that sharing. The conscientious teacher will consider such questions as the following when choosing poetry to share:

[3] *Every Time I Climb a Tree.* Vigorous and direct, McCord's poetry gives us unique views of commonplace things and events, illustrated boldly by Marc Simont. Also try *For Me to Say* and *Take Sky.*

[4] "Mick," about Reeves's mongrel dog, is one of many poems by different poets included in Geoffrey Palmer and Noel Lloyd, eds., *Round About Eight.* Bold black line and limited color are used in the casual yet effective illustrations. Reeves's poetry is collected in *Blackbird in the Lilac.*

[5] *The Golden Hive.* From the insignificant beetles clad in green metallic armor of the first poem to the majestic Blackfoot chieftains clad in quilled and beaded hides, described in the last poem, the collection offers much of interest to boys. See also *The Wizard in the Well.*

- *Is the poem something I can read effectively?*
  We have all had the experience of hearing or
  reading a poem, and knowing that it was by an
  important poet—but *we* still didn't like it! As
  you search for poetry to share with children, if
  you come across something you're tempted to
  share because it's topical or by a famous poet,
  make sure you like it yourself. If you don't, you
  won't be able to read it well. A good test is to
  ask yourself if you would feel self-conscious reading the poem to an adult. Though its intended
  audience is children, not an adult, the question
  is important. If you would feel self-conscious
  reading the poem to an adult, choose a different
  poem.
- *Is the poem different in form or content from
  other things I've shared recently?* We all do have
  preferences, however unexamined they are. We
  need to look analytically at what we choose to
  make sure we present a wide variety, not only of
  ideas,[6] but also of styles (unrhymed, cinquains,
  free verse, septolets, and others).
- *Is it a poem which will appeal to both girls and
  boys?* [7] This is especially important, since collections of poetry are apt to contain many poems
  more likely to appeal to girls, both because of
  topic and treatment. Watch carefully that the
  sweet, cute, or elaborately descriptive poem in

[6] And the ideas don't always have to be serious! A delightful collection
of assorted absurdities, the poems in Louis Untermeyer, ed., *The Golden
Book of Fun and Nonsense,* provide a pleasant change from more serious
poetry.

[7] Some suggestions are included in Ruth Hartley, "Poetry for Boys in
Primary Grades," *Elementary English,* Dececmber 1972, pp. 1153–57. The
author comments on the frequency with which poetry is considered non-
masculine and boys' resultant dislike for it. She then suggests specific poems
and approaches that should result in changes.

which little happens doesn't overbalance other
images. Children, boys and girls, are interested
in poems which present a clear and unusual view,
or poems in which something active happens.

• *Have I included poetry by children, as well as
adult poets?* It is possible to respond positively
to this question today, as there are increasing
numbers of anthologies of poetry by children
available. These include poetry by children from
other countries,[8] and by minority-group children.[9] Exposure to such poetry gives added di-
mension to children's understanding of the range
of poetry. It further instills the concept that
poetry is a form that children can write ex-
pressively.

SHARING POETRY WITH CHILDREN

There is something particularly captivating to children
when the teacher has a poem to share immediately following
a group experience. When an excited class of first graders
tumbles into the room from recess, following a child cup-
ping a caterpillar in his or her hand, it is time for "The
Caterpillar," by Christina Rossetti.[10] Similarly, when the
fifth grade children's attention is drawn from the math lesson by the lonely cry of Canadian geese, cutting a heavy

---

[8] See Richard Lewis, comp., *Miracles,* or idem, *The Wind and the Rain.*
Collections of poems from children of many lands are enhanced by sensitively designed formats that make the books poetic and visual delights.

[9] Of the many collections now available, Kenneth Koch, *Wishes, Lies and
Dreams* is typical. See also Stephen M. Joseph, *The Me Nobody Knows,* or
Cornish and Dixon, *Chicory.*

[10] Included in Louis Untermeyer, ed., *The Golden Treasury of Poetry,*
p. 73. Later in the year, after you have been successful in nurturing the
caterpillar through its cocoon stage into butterfly brilliance, read May
Swenson, "Was Worm," ibid., p. 73. The unique view of the poet is
enhanced by the unconventional form of the poem.

wedge through iron gray clouds, then is the time for "Something Told the Wild Geese," by Rachel Field.[11] At such times as these the immediacy of the experience and the ability of the teacher to quickly link memorable words to a memorable experience is important. Such linking builds an interest in poetry and an awareness that poets have caught an ephemeral experience in words that can be savored again and again.

At such times, the teacher must be able to go quickly and unobtrusively to a source for the poem, find it, and share it with children. For this reason many teachers keep an ever-increasing poetry file box with poems grouped by topic. Poems can be attached to recipe cards for permanence and filed according to topic in order to be immediately available. In addition to this approach some teachers like to use margin tabs in anthologies they own, making it possible to turn quickly to appropriate poems.

Beyond such utilitarian, incidental use of poetry to intensify an experience, the teacher should also plan an organized sequence of poems to share throughout the year. This broadly based sequence could be called the poetry curriculum. It is designed to acquaint children with a wider range of poetry than is possible in incidental sharing.

Probably reading a poem a day provides a good prepared environment in which children can write poetry. If a classroom teacher reads just one poem each school day, children will be exposed to over a hundred poems during a year. Some of these will make deep, lasting impressions; others will be as ephemeral as the wind, forgotten before the day is over. This need not make the teacher uneasy, knowing that in a program of such extensive sharing of poetry, each child is sure to find something of deep individual meaning.

Another approach to structuring a poetry curriculum is to feature a *Poet of the Month*. One kindergarten teacher

[11] Included in May Hill Arbuthnot, ed., *The Arbuthnot Anthology*, p. 187.

has planned her poetry experience to intensively acquaint the children with the work of a few poets, using many poems by one author during a month. For example, the teacher might use David McCord as poet of the month, presenting an impressional treatment of him as an introduction, talking briefly with the children about the poet, his life and work. A bulletin board might feature a picture of the poet.[12] The teacher then shares many poems with the children during that month, including various poets, but concentrating on the featured poet's work. Part of the sharing in class includes eliciting children's reactions to what they like about a poem. The poetry books should be left at the book table for children to look at in their leisure time. Children of kindergarten age cannot read the books themselves, but they seem to enjoy returning to the books and looking at the illustrations that remind them of poems already heard. As the month goes on, some of the poems children especially enjoyed are repeated upon their request. This repetition leads to some informal learning of poems, though no emphasis is put on formal memorization.

READING EFFECTIVELY

There are many ways to plan a curriculum in poetry. Such organized sharing presupposes that the teacher can read poetry effectively; to do so requires practice. Poetry is more difficult to read than prose because it is more condensed; nuances of meaning are often expressed more subtly than in prose. In addition, minor changes in paralinguistic elements of pitch, stress, and juncture signal meaning more elusively than is true in prose.

This means that teachers interested in reading poetry

[12] Trade-book publishers will often supply bibliographic information, including a picture, in leaflet format about their children's poets and authors. Write directly to the publisher with such a request.

effectively will practice different ways of interpreting a poem. After choosing a poem, practice reading it several times, varying pitch (the pattern on high and low sounds), stress (the pattern of emphasis), and juncture (the pattern of pauses and complete stops). It is helpful to mark the *thought units* in a poem, which often do not coincide with the printed lines. One of the most common problems in reading poetry aloud is stopping at the end of lines, rather than at the end of the thought units.

You might even find it useful to record the poem on tape or cassette in order to listen to how you sound to children. Few of us have the objectivity necessary to hear our voices as others hear them. A few analytic sessions with a tape recorder can improve most teachers' poetry reading skills.

All of the above may indeed sound time-consuming. Teachers may wonder to what end all this selection and preparation time is being recommended. Development of an appreciation of poetry takes time; results of this planning, selection, and sharing are sometimes not readily apparent. Yet such a diversified experience with poetry is important in getting children to write poetry. Perhaps with such a thoughtful approach to poetry, it is possible to replace the misconceptions mentioned earlier with some more helpful conceptions about poetry. Long-range goals of a poetry program might include the establishment of the following conceptions about poetry.

Conception One

Poetry expresses how we feel. Children need to understand that poets have used poetry to express deeply felt emotions in concise ways that communicate meaningfully to audiences. When Mary O'Neill writes about the word *forget* and likens it to a hider in a long black cape, she starts us on a compelling journey toward that memorable last line:

"Nothing that happens goes truly away . . ." [13] The power in that line shows us how far poetry goes beyond being simply "pretty." Poets have cast innumerable shades of feeling into poetry. Some of these are feelings children have also had; others are feelings children may not yet have experienced directly. Contact with poetry helps children reflect on their own feelings and share vicariously what others have felt.

Conception Two

Poetry often gives us a unique view of something ordinary. It is true that poets sometimes deal with extraordinary events. But a distinguishing quality of poetry is that poets can make us see something commonplace in a new way. This might be an experience, an object, a feeling, or a sensory input. Because of this experience with poetry, we can perceive our world, its objects, occupants, and events in new and more sensitive ways.

Conception Three

Poetry is multiple. We have been talking about "Poetry is. . . ." Perhaps "Poetry are . . ." would be a more accurate way of expressing the idea that poetry encompasses a vast array of forms and styles, of models and meters. It is crucial that children be helped to understand that poetry forms are limitless. Too often children leave elementary school thinking that end rhymes and insistent rhythmic "thump" are inevitable concomitants of poetry. Broadening children's exposure to a multiplicity of forms will help them understand

[13] "Forget," in *Words Words Words,* pp. 40–41. Some of the poems, for example "The Consonants and the Vowels" and the ones on punctuation, are primarily didactic and quite forgettable. Others in which the poet explores shades of meaning are evocative explorations. "Hope," and "Gossamer" are worthy of much rereading.

that they needn't try to communicate their ideas in conventional *abab* form.

Much of the foregoing may seem somewhat unrelated to having children write poetry. Yet a crucial factor in encouraging children to write is the preparatory environment a teacher creates. A rich and continual immersion in poetry is an indispensable preparation for actual composition experiences.

WRITING EXPERIENCES

All of the foregoing contacts with poetry could be justified in the curriculum on the basis of the aesthetic experience they provide. In addition, however, such experiences are highly utilitarian in establishing an environment that encourages children to write poetry.

To describe comprehensively ways in which children can be motivated to write poetry is beyond the scope of one chapter. Several complete books are available that do this quite effectively.[14] Rather, we will consider the way children whose writing is included in this book were helped to write poetry. After such initial sharing experiences as those described earlier, children were asked to write poetry. The children were given experiences in writing structured, unrhymed poetry, including such forms as haiku, cinquain, and diamante. There are two reasons why these types of poetry are effective with children:

- They provide a structure or organization within which children can compose. Children seem to need some structure, and these forms are easily

[14] See Flora J. Arnstein, *Poetry and the Child,* or Mauree Applegate, *When the Teacher Says, "Write a Poem,"* or Nina Willis Walter, *Let Them Write Poetry.*

learned and facilitative if not applied too rigorously.

- They are unrhymed, which means children do not need to be concerned with attempting to fit thoughts to specific words. Rather, children search for the most effective words to express their thoughts, a more logical writing problem.

THE PROBLEM OF RHYME

Experts on poetry writing concur that rhyme should be minimized in composition experiences for children. Many years ago Mearns said:

> Rhyme is a marvelous but unnecessary ornament; a great thing, no mistake, when done by expert artists, but a weak thing and an obstruction of the spirit oftentimes in the hands of any but a technician.[15]

More recently an American authority on children's poetry writing, Nancy Larrick, stated:

> At no time did we suggest the use of rhyme. In fact, we discouraged attempts at rhyming lines because at this stage rhyme seems to force a child into goose-step thinking.[16]

Such feelings are shared by the British author Sybil Marshall, whose book reveals a remarkable sensitivity to children and their composition abilities. She has said:

> Attempts to rhyme were never forbidden, though I was always chary of them, because of the feeling

[15] Hughes Mearns, *Creative Power*, p. 77.
[16] *Green is Like a Meadow of Grass*, p. 63.

that the use of both rhythm and rhyme would result in a kind of forced cleverness, or else degenerate into sheer doggerel.[17]

HAIKU

Many children enjoy responding to the challenge of composing haiku, a seventeen-syllable, three-line Japanese form of poetry. The first line usually has five syllables; the second, seven; and the third, five. Haiku is frequently marked by a strong nature theme and often contains seasonal references. There are many books available to use in introducing the form to children.[18] In addition, various language-arts series introduce the form.[19]

The caution to remember in introducing this form is the need for flexibility. It is important to introduce the form accurately, pointing out to children the required number of syllables and lines. Yet, it is equally important to remember that this requirement was for poetry written in the original Japanese language, *not* English. Because of this, children should be encouraged to notice that in translation the number of syllables is sometimes more or less than seventeen.

In writing the form, children must be allowed freedom in meeting the syllable requirement. While seventeen is the desired number, children must know that this is a flexible

[17] *An Experiment in Education,* p. 165.

[18] You can begin with very young children, using Richard Lewis, ed., *In a Spring Garden.* The collage illustrations by Ezra Jack Keats are boldly simple and elegant accompaniments to the haiku verses. For older children the books by Harold Henderson are useful. See *Haiku in English* or *An Introduction to Haiku.*

[19] See, for example, H. Thompson Fillmer et al., *Patterns of Language,* bk. 6, pp. 250–51, 261. Or see John S. Hand et al., *Progress in English,* bk. 4, pp. 204–5; bk. 6, pp. 94–95. Or see Cornelia Nachbar et al., *Flying Free,* bk. 6, pp. 10–12.

requirement. Perhaps saying exactly what *they* want to say in a poem will require more or less syllables.

One teacher tried using this form with her children. She planned an initial motivation session in which she showed slides of nature scenes while reading haiku.[20] A discussion following the reading led children to an understanding of the form, its syllable requirements, and the usual nature or seasonal theme. With this as a basis, children composed the following haiku.

The mountain with its
glimmering ledges and cliffs
shines in the moonlight.

by Mike

The cotton fields wave
at the soft shimmering sun
above the sky.

by Denise

Oh, little green snake
you always make the earth shake
scaring all the girls.

by Tom

Like a bright diamond
glossy, more precious than gold
A simple, lost star.

by Greg

[20] Among the books she used were the following: Sylvia Cassedy and Kunihiro Suetake, *Birds, Frogs, and Moonlight.* A brief introductory essay on the nature of haiku opens this well-designed book. Each double-page spread includes four elements: a bold black-line and color-wash drawing, the haiku written in English, in Japanese, and in calligraphy. Harry Behn, *Cricket Songs.* Small, black and white photographs of original Japanese art are interspersed with haiku by many of the better-known Japanese poets.

Oh dreadful lightning!
Why must you burn my house down
and leave me so cold?

by Jerry

An expanded form, *tanka*, requires the addition of two seven-syllable lines at the end, for a total of thirty-one syllables. This form is described more completely by Wolsch.[21]

CINQUAIN

Another relatively simple, yet structured form, cinquain, should be part of a poetry-writing curriculum for children. There are few book collections of cinquains for children,[22] though poems by the American inventor of this form can be used.[23] Several articles offer detailed descriptions of teaching techniques,[24] and some elementary language series introduce the form.[25]

Cinquain, like haiku, is a syllabic form of verse, but the pattern involves a gradual building up of syllables to eight in a line and then a return to two. The lines are organized:

[21] Robert A. Wolsch, *Poetic Composition Through the Grades*. The author describes the process and values of poetic composition, showing with accounts of classroom projects how teachers help children achieve creative expression.

[22] A happy exception to this rule is Lee Bennett Hopkins, comp., *City Talk*. Striking black and white photographs illustrate this collection of forty-two cinquains written by urban children.

[23] Poems by Adelaid Crapsey and a detailed biographical account of her life are included in Lee Bennett Hopkins, "From Trudeau's Garden," *Elementary English*, October 1967, pp. 613–14.

[24] You will find very helpful suggestions in Lee Bennett Hopkins, "For Creative Fun, Let Them Try a Cinquain," *Grade Teacher*, December 1966, pp. 83ff.

[25] See Fillmer et al., *Patterns of Language*, bk. 4, p. 115. Or see Hand et al., *Progress in English*, bk. 6, pp. 96–97.

_____2 syllables
_____4 syllables
_____6 syllables
_____8 syllables
_____2 syllables

The pattern as expressed in verse:

First Sign

I see . . .
the pale snowdrop,
bravely seeking the sun.
Be gone, winter winds: stay away—
It's spring.

Children seem to enjoy writing cinquains. The following are typical of the writing they can do in this form:

Skylab.
Flying, testing,
Staying in a steady orbit.
Staying up in a sky orbit,
Trying.

by Paul

Grass snake.
Little squiggly thing
Creeping along the ground.
Giant boy tries to catch the snake,
Poor thing!

by Tom

I see
you little bee,
gathering nectar from
flowers to make honey for us.
Thank you.

by Robin

Who is
the man in the
white silk suit and brown shoes
drinking from the water fountain
neatly?

                              by Keith

Gray colt
loosely running
Nickering playfully
for his playmate, a dark filly
to come.

                              by Kathy

Rabbit
runs away from
animals that chase him.
He would like to climb a tree but
he can't.

                              by Jeff

One teacher, working with fourth and sixth grade children, alters the form somewhat and finds the changes result in a successful poetry experience. She recommends the following pattern:

First line—one word, giving the title.
Second line—two words, describing the title.
Third line—three words, expressing an action.
Fourth line—four words, expressing a feeling, and
Fifth line—another word for the title.

In her article, the author tells how she uses this pattern and describes her instructional strategies, which result in the effective poems she includes.[26]

[26] Jennie T. Dearmin, "Teaching Your Children to Paint Pictures with Words," *Grade Teacher*, March 1965, pp. 26–27.

Elaboration of the form into chain and double cinquains are described in the work of Ruth Kearney Carlson, a prolific author long known for her concern about children's composition.[27]

DIAMANTE

This is a syllabic, structured form created by a professor interested in helping children express themselves in poetry.[28] The article describes in detail the form and also approaches for encouraging children to write diamante. In form the poem is diamond shaped, composed of seven lines as follows:

1 word: subject noun
2 words: adjectives
3 words: participles (-ing, -ed)
4 words: nouns related to subject
3 words: participles
2 words: adjectives
1 word: noun (opposite of subject)

Children seem to find this form helpful in writing poetry. One child wrote about Christmas:

Ornament
Glistening, bright
Hanging, sparkling, falling
Tinsel, popcorn, lights, star
Shining, breaking, cracked
Wrecked, ruined
Star.

by Lori

[27] *Sparkling Words*, pp. 130–31. The author presents an extended section on poetry, describing such forms as the septet, lanterne, lai verse, and triolet. In addition to description of the forms, the author includes many samples written by children.

[28] Iris M. Tiedt, "A New Poetry Form: The Diamante," in *Elementary English*, May 1969, pp. 588–89.

Fifth grade children wrote the following:

Football
Rough, tough
Passing, catching, kicking
Goal,   yard,   paddle,   table
Running, hitting, serving
exciting, tiring
Ping Pong.

by Steve

Mini-bike
Fast, complicated
shifting, speeding, moving
lights, battery, clutch, cylinders
Sitting, steering, cornering
Luxurious, enclosed
Car.

by Fred

Cats
Nice   kind
playing, walking, running
tail,   four legs,   paws,   fur
eating, licking, drinking
mean,   rough
Dogs

by Diana

Fat
Plump, chubby
Eating, talking, jiggling
belly,   cheeks,   arms,   legs
slimming, dieting, lengthening
graceful,   bony
thin

by Andy

Games
Fun, cheerful
Playing, tackling, fighting
man,   enemy,   guns,   blood
killing, screaming, exploding
fierce, bloody
War.

by Doug

During a diamante-writing session, sixth graders wrote:

Water
hot,   cold
dripping, dropping, plunging
rain,   oceans,   lakes,   rivers
pouring, splashing, sprinkling
soft,   hard
sand

by Steven

Animals
shy,   proud
scurrying, hopping, jumping
families,   homes,   food,   children
hurrying, playing, hunting
busy,   needy
man

by Molly

OTHER SYLLABIC FORMS

There are many other structured forms that facilitate poetry writing. These are described in detail by Carlson. A sept is a

syllabic arrangement as follows: 1, 2, 3, 4, 3, 2, 1. A sixth
grade child wrote:

> Deer
> jumping
> running fast,
> long striding leaps
> dash away—
> away
> fast.
>
> by Tom

In a septet, the pattern is: 3, 5, 7, 9, 7, 5, 3. One sixth
grade child wrote the following modified septet:

> Smart raccoons
> Washing away dirt
> on their food before eating.
> Then hungrily the masked animals
> gulp down the cleaned food
> carelessly.
>
> by Kathy

A lanterne is based on a syllable scheme of 1, 2, 3, 4, 1.

> Dolls
> old and
> worn away
> with love sit and
> wait.
>
> by Julie

Finally, a vignette is based on a syllable plan of 2, 4, 4, 6,
7, 3. Sixth grade children wrote:

Cricket
you chirp all night
by the silver
moon—chirping loud, breaking
the silence of the dark night.
Chirp, chirp, chirp.

by Jim

Who likes
the small earthworm
wriggling through
the dark moldy soil
cleaning it, and making it
good for plants?

by Keith

CONCRETE POETRY

Another form children should experience is concrete poetry, which must be seen to be appreciated. In this form, the way words and phrases are arranged on the paper is an important elaboration of the meaning, for the words look like the idea expressed. The form is not a new one. Such writers as Lewis Carroll have used it.[29] A helpful book to use in introducing the form is now available.[30] In addition, if children seem particularly interested in the form, and teachers want to work extensively with it, they can refer to a tastefully de-

[29] See the mouse tail/tale in Martin Gardner, ed., *The Annotated Alice*. With the original illustrations by John Tenniel, this exhaustively annotated volume is a handsome guide to the complexities of Carroll.

[30] A. Barbara Pilon, *Concrete Is Not Always Hard*. The brief introductory section containing suggestions for teachers is helpful, and the bulk of the book is made up of poetry drawn from a variety of sources, including some fine ones by the author.

signed book that will augment understanding of words expressing their ideas visually.[31]

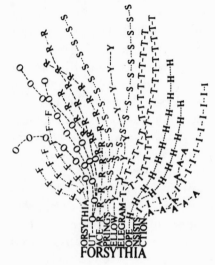

Mary Ellen Solt

EVALUATION IN POETRY

Poetry, a more ephemeral form than prose, is more difficult to evaluate. Response to poetry and inclination to write it seem to wither more quickly than response to and writing of prose. Because of this, teachers must approach evaluation in poetry with a more gentle hand than they do with evaluation of prose. Nonetheless, there are ways teachers can evaluate the poetry experiences they provide for children and the children's success in expressing themselves in poetry.

The primary evaluation attempts are devoted to determin-

[31] John Cataldo, *Words and Calligraphy for Children.* This lavishly illustrated record of ways words and art materials can be unified into visual expressions contains examples of work by children from six to seventeen. It suggests many practical projects with which to involve children with visual forms of words and letters.

ing if children are still responding positively to poetry. As teachers read and occasionally discuss poetry with the children, they must be constantly alert for signs of boredom or disinterest. Keeping in mind the misconceptions about poetry described earlier, teachers should examine the poems chosen to make sure they are not inadvertently furthering these misconceptions. Every effort should be made to ensure that poems shared with children are appropriate to the interests and cognitive understanding of the group in addition to being good poetry. The question teachers must consider with regularity is: *Do the children still seem to like poetry?* That subjective question is difficult to answer, of course, for the most stoic and unresponsive child may be responding internally with warmth and delight. The child responding most overtly may be seeking teacher approval rather than displaying genuine interest. Despite these problems, the teacher should keep reassessing the answer to the above question, realizing that if receptive channels can be kept open, children's ability to respond to poetry may lead to poetry writing.

Another type of evaluation occurs as the teacher reads the poetry the children have written. In examining these poems, the teacher looks consciously for answers to such questions as these:

- Does the topic the child chose to write about seem to be a logical choice for the child? For example, fourth grade boys seldom choose to write about the exhilaration they feel about signs of spring. Assuming that children are allowed to choose their topic, does the choice seem to be one the child wanted to make, or was it one designed to win approval from the teacher? The goal here is to reinforce the idea that, to be significant, the

poem must be about a topic of genuine concern
to the child.

- Is there a word or phrase that you can commend
to the child and to the other children? It is important to look for the unusual word choice or
an unusual use of a common word. Seek out an
unusual phrase and ask the child to read his or
her poem so the other children can enjoy it.

- Does the topic seem to be treated honestly, within
the context of the situation? That is a subjective
judgment, of course, and not one that necessarily
needs to be conveyed to the child. If you discover
a poem written by one of your children that is full
of ideas and expressions that are stilted and artificial, perhaps you need to reexamine the environment for poetry writing you have provided.

- Is there an unusual perception of a commonplace
object or event? One of the conceptions about
poetry worth instilling was mentioned earlier:
Poetry gives us a unique view of the commonplace. Very young children view the world with
a freshness that often amazes adults. Our job as
teachers of poetry is to preserve this freshness of
vision as children grow older.

- Does the poem tell us something about how the
child felt or reacted? Beyond simply giving us
information about how an object looked or felt
or smelled, does the poem also include some indication of the child's reaction to the object or
event being described?

Beyond looking simply at individual poems, however, the
teacher carefully examines children's responses to the act of
writing poetry. In attempting to build a year-long poetry

experience for children, the teacher reflects upon the answers to such questions as:

- Are children becoming more willing to express themselves in poetic form? Are more of the children in the room choosing to respond in poetry when a writing assignment doesn't specify what literary genre is to be used? Often a room may have one child particularly gifted in poetry. What a delight! The goal, however, is to increase *all* children's ability to respond in poetry.
- Are children becoming more able to express themselves in different kinds of poetry? The three types of poetry receiving major consideration in this chapter—haiku, cinquain, and diamante—are structured forms that seem to facilitate writing. They are, however, only a beginning. Children need to be exposed to, and challenged to write, many different types of poetry. Not all of these forms will appeal to all children, but a way to evaluate the effectiveness of the poetry program is to consider the ease with which children express themselves in different poetry forms.

In this, as in other areas of the writing program, progress in developing writing competency is slow. Nonetheless, teachers interested in promoting the goal of this writing program—better writers and writing—do evaluate. They evaluate both the success of the programs planned and the success individual children had in a particular poetry-writing assignment. Only by doing both can they continue to shape and reshape the poetry program to make it more effective.

8

RESHAPING
WRITING

Is it not the business of education to improve ability, to add to strength, to secure superior results? [1]

After children have written their ideas in prose or poetry,
what happens? What do we, as teachers, do with children to
help them improve their writing ability, to achieve the
superior results of which Mearns wrote so many years ago?
   There are two common approaches used by teachers to
help children gain the strength in writing that is their potential. The first approach emphasizes spontaneous creativity.
Teachers, especially at the primary level, who feel that the
creativity of the child's work must not be tampered with,
often maintain that nothing beyond initial writing should
be done. Carlson, as an example of experts who espouse this
point of view, speaks of the flickering flame of creativity,
which teachers must be careful not to extinguish. [2] The child
has expressed himself and the result is creative; to ask a
child to change or alter the results of the creative process is

[1] Hughes Mearns, *Creative Power*, p. 43.
[2] Ruth Kearney Carlson, *Sparkling Words*.

a mistake.[3] Such teachers happily accept the child's efforts, praising unusual word choices, figures of speech, or original ideas. Stories are shared orally and enjoyed briefly as the ephemeral things they are before work is begun on new stories.

The assumption made in this approach is that writing will improve as the child matures. A fairly typical statement by proponents of such a program is:

> From further opportunities to compose . . . and from much exposure . . . to literature, more extended, stronger writing will almost certainly ensue. [4]

The question that may be raised is: *Does* such stronger writing ensue as the child matures? Perhaps it does for some children; whether it does for most children is debatable.

Another approach is also common. This could be called the "compulsive-corrector" syndrome and is unfortunately pervasive. It is the antithesis of the first approach. After children have written in response to some motivation, they are called upon to make the mechanical corrections that will render their papers easy to read. Painstaking attention to correct spelling, placement of punctuation, capitalization, and paragraph or sentence faults is characteristic of this approach. The assumption made in this approach is that if attention is given to the mechanical aspects of writing, "better" writing will result. The great number of adults who resist any efforts to put pen to paper for even a simple letter would seem to indicate the ineffectiveness of this approach.

---

[3] Another expert, Ruth G. Strickland, states that writing is finished ". . . and is satisfactory when he [the child] is satisfied with it." *The Language Arts in the Elementary School*, p. 343.

[4] Alvina T. Burrows, Dianne L. Monson, and Russell G. Stauffer, *New Horizons in the Language Arts*, p. 192.

If neither of these approaches is maximally effective in helping children reach their writing potential, what is an alternative?

A NEW APPROACH

The approach suggested in this chapter differs from both of the above approaches. It is different from the first approach in that it requires that children look at and think about their writing after the initial process is complete. It is different from the second approach in that it emphasizes a reshaping of content that results when children look thoughtfully at the *ideas* included in their writing rather than at cosmetic aspects of how the paper looks.

The assumption made in this program is that writing is a skill that can be developed. Certainly it is a skill not devoid of art; in all skills there is a place for individuality, creativity, and unique expression of ideas. But writing is a skill that can be likened to the skill of listening. We don't assume that listening skills will automatically improve. Rather, we show children how to improve their ability in this area. The highest levels of listening include much creativity. Similarly in writing, we take children's natural ability and interest and show them how they can improve their ability.

To help children become better writers, thus able to produce more effective writing, we ask them to engage in a process that few elementary schoolchildren now encounter. This process is called reshaping, or *editing*.

In chapter one, two different types of editing were described. The first of these, *concurrent editing,* is that intuitive process by which writers make choices of words, phrases, sentences, relationships, and sequence *as* they write down their ideas. An internal thought process, often not apparent to an observer, it is individual choice making in the act of composition. As such, and rightly, it is not a concern of the teacher.

The second type of editing *is* of concern to the teacher, however. Called *completion editing,* it is a conscious process one can learn, which results in improved writing. It is a crucial step in the journey toward effective writing, as children develop the ability to look analytically at what they have written. In doing so, children develop the ability to discern what is strong and should be retained and what is less strong and should be reshaped. Using the term *editing* as synonymous with *reshaping,* however, necessitates a caution.

Editing is used to mean content, or thought, modification, *not* mechanical correction. This is using the term in a different way than many experts about writing have used the term. One author suggests having children "who are skillful at using punctuation, capitalization and writing mechanics . . . act as editors. [5] This is *not* editing, but rather simple correcting. It represents one reason why children have such negative attitudes toward doing anything with their writing once the first draft is finished. The emphasis is too frequently on this sort of mechanical correcting rather than on more meaningful content reorganization. A basic feature of this program is a deeper meaning to the use of the term *editing.*

WHY RESHAPE WRITING?

To justify the process of reshaping writing, or editing, the major purpose of this writing program must be repeated. The purpose is to help children write better, to produce more effective writing. If we are going to justify the inclu-

[5] James A. Smith, *Creative Teaching of the Language Arts in the Elementary School,* p. 296.

sion of large blocks of time devoted to writing, results must point to the effectiveness of the time spent. Particularly in an age when accountability is a crucial word, we must be able to point to the results of what we do with children.

A caution about results must be included here. The results of an elementary school writing program are not apparent at the end of a semester or year. The final evaluation of a writing program cannot be made until children leave the elementary school. It is true that along the way individual pieces of writing of great beauty, unusual perception, or unique statement may be uncovered and shared. Like experiences in creative drama, however, the impact of the writing program cannot be fully assessed until children have completed the program.

Reshaping is offered, then, as a way to help children become better writers. It is further offered as a more realistic approach in that it bears greater resemblance to the way in which adult writers work. In the process of looking at their own writing, examining it to determine where *they* want to make changes or alterations, children can become better writers. In addressing themselves to the questions described in following sections of this chapter, they learn to become analytic about their writing and interested in the process of improving what they wrote.

A more mature understanding of the writing process and how adult writers work will also result. There are very few adult writers who write a first draft that is also a final draft, as children are asked to do in the first approach described above. Similarly, there are almost no writers who write a first draft and then devote their attention solely to mechanical corrections, as in the second approach described above. So both of these approaches are unrealistic in helping children understand the process of writing. Instead, the process of reshaping, or editing, which is described here, is the more realistic approach, both for the improved writing ability that results and for the increased understanding of the process that results.

HOW TO RESHAPE [6]

How do teachers encourage children to reshape their writing, to look at the ideas included and make them more effective? The key to this part of the writing program is the teachers' ability to ask questions. They must be able to look at what the children have written and ask the appropriate questions that will help the children consider their writing. Such questions as these will encourage children to analyze the writing to determine what parts of it are fine and strong and need no more work, and what parts are less well done and could profit from more thought.

Just as we have worked throughout the program with specific assignments designed to encourage children to think about aspects of writing, so the editing questions need to be very specific. With the youngest children these are asked in ways that will initiate the process in a painless, non-threatening way. With a group of young children we begin with simple questions:

- What part of our story do you like best? Can you tell us why?
- Is there a part of our story you would like to change?
- Which of the words in the story are most interesting to you? Why do you notice them as you read the story?
- Which one of the characters is most interesting to you? Can you tell us why?

[6] For another statement about editing see Bernarr Folta, *Three Strategies for Revising Sentences*. Folta's concern, rhetorical improvement, has to do with three processes: elimination, substitution, and addition.

In dealing with children's responses to such questions, as well as to any questions asked about writing, teachers must be careful to develop the idea that these are questions to which there is *no* one right answer. By the way in which a teacher encourages each child to respond and the way in which each response is accepted, the teacher reinforces the idea that the question can elicit many answers. It is especially important that the teacher avoid conveying to children, no matter how subtly, his or her own response to the question. Certainly some of the answers will be more perceptive than others, reflecting differences in children's thinking ability or maturity. Nonetheless, the purpose of this questioning is to develop habits of reflecting upon, thinking about, and reacting to written material. Each child will develop this ability at his or her own level. Some will become very adept at it; others will have less success. The questioning does not become an end in itself but rather a means of encouraging this reflective attitude toward writing.

WHEN TO BEGIN

Often the idea of reshaping writing seems to be a rather complicated idea, beyond the grasp or interest of most elementary children. Such is not the case if the answers to two questions are considered perceptively. The first of these is: *When* can editing begin? The second is: *How much* editing should occur?

The answer to the first question is, as early as first grade children can understand the idea of adding to, or changing, what they have written. In many of these early group-writing endeavors, the teacher has provided an experience, and children are asked to dictate their response to it. Such group-chart stories are a sound way to begin writing, because:

- They help children understand that writing is a three-step process—a "taking-in," a "giving-out," and a reshaping. In the first, writers take in some motivation or stimulus, which makes them want to write. In the second, they give out their ideas, or response to the motivation, in written form. Third, they look at what they have written and reform it to say more effectively what they want to say. This three-step process is typical of writing, whether one is thinking of a group of pre-school children dictating a story or an adult author writing.
- They help children understand that writing should be based on experience. At the beginning levels of this program, the experiences will be immediate and physical; at later levels, the experiences will be with literature.

An example of how one teacher uses this process with children may help clarify the kind of work young children can accomplish. In this case, the stories were dictated by a group of children in early November of their first grade year in school. An experience in the classroom resulted in the following story:

A tadpole!
He is growing legs.
Look at it wiggle!
Michael can pet it.

This group-chart story was written after children had been encouraged to observe the tadpole during the week it was in their room. Several days after they had written the story, the teacher asked them to think about it together. Her questions were very simple:

- Is there anything else we can tell the reader?
- Can we add anything to make our story more interesting?

The following changes resulted:

A big, black tadpole!
He is growing skinny frog legs.
Look at it wiggle in the water.
Michael can pet it.

This illustrates the way in which even young children can look at their work and reshape or edit it. Two things are apparent in comparing the versions. First, the reshaping in this case consists entirely of *adding* to the original story. This is to be expected with young children, for it is far more difficult to delete something one has written than to add to it. It takes much maturity to pencil out a sentence one has labored on. So the teacher is, at this stage of development, pleased with the additions to the writing, knowing that deletions will become easier later.

Second, not every sentence is reshaped. The last line remains the same in the second version. This, too, is fine. The teacher keeps in mind that, though all sentences *can* be reshaped, not all sentences *should* be reshaped. The teacher who worked with these children did not try to push them to add something to every sentence. When they came to the last sentence, the children did not care to add anything, and the teacher respected their judgment.

The following story was done two weeks later by the same group of first grade children. In this case, the reshaping included the addition of several descriptive sentences. The first writing included only two sentences:

A grasshopper!
I got one!

Not terribly inspired writing, though it was indeed strongly felt by the children, who had with vigor chased the grasshoppers that had gotten loose in the room. Several days later, the teacher again asked the children to look at their writing. The group then came up with this edited version:

A green grasshopper!
He has long, thin legs.
He has a huge, yellowish body.
He can fly with see-through wings.
I got one!

In this case, as in the first, the reshaping consisted entirely of adding to the original story. The additions here are more extensive and, again, primarily descriptive. Only one sentence remains the same as in the original version. Through judicious questioning about the nature of the grasshopper and what it could do, the teacher helped the group to a more effective piece of writing than the original simple declaration of what happened.

Deletion in writing is more difficult to achieve, for what children have written is very important to them, as it is to adults. Children's stories thus are often full of irrelevant or redundant details that clutter up the writing.[7] The teacher will want to help children achieve the maturity and objectivity about writing that will allow them to consider: "Is there anyplace where we can leave something out?" or "Is there anyplace we can combine two sentences into one?"

The first grade that dictated the previous stories was beginning to develop such abilities when they wrote the following stories two months later. In their first version there were opportunities for editing. The story was originally dictated:

[7] See the comment about this in Alvina T. Burrows et al., *They All Want to Write*, p. 203.

A Winter Walk
It didn't feel like winter, so we went for a walk.
We saw a giant puddle that was melting.
It was ice that was melting.
We saw tire marks in the mud.
There were bird's nests up in the trees.
We jumped puddles and looked at streams of water.
Then we played a game on the playground.
It was a nice sunny winter afternoon.

The teacher purposely did no editing immediately follow-ing the initial composition session. Wisely, she turned to other things for a while, hoping the children could later look more objectively at what they had written. Four days later, the children reread their story to determine how they could make it "better." Through thoughtful questioning, the teacher led the group to the following edited version:

A Winter Walk
It didn't feel like winter, so we went for a walk.
We saw a giant puddle that was ice melting.
We saw wet tire marks in the mushy brown mud.
There were old bird's nests up in the tall trees.
We jumped over muddy puddles, and looked at icy
    streams of water.
Then we played a game on the playground.
It was a nice sunny winter afternoon.

As in earlier stories, there were some sentences—the first and the last two—that remained exactly the same. The chil-dren continued to add descriptive words to make their writ-ing more vivid. Sentences four through six of the original were enhanced in editing by the addition of descriptive words.

However, an additional editing ability appeared. The children were now able to take two sentences (sentences two and three in the original version) and combine them to make one sentence, which still retained the original content. This represented another step forward. The two sentences in the original said essentially the same thing. Combining them made for more compact, and thus more effective, writing.

Rearranging sequences in stories is also an important editing skill. In the following pair of stories from the same first grade, we see children continuing to combine sentences, eliminating some unnecessary words. In addition, we see them beginning to make decisions about relocating sentences for greater effectiveness. The original story:

> The iguana lives on the ground. He lives in the trees.
> It eats vegetables and flowers. He lives in Mexico.
> He runs away from danger and hides under weeds in the water.
> He jumps very far from tree to tree. He lives in the desert.

The editing resulted in the following story:

> The iguana lives on the ground and in the trees.
> It eats vegetables and flowers.
> He runs away from danger by jumping from tree to tree.
> Sometimes he dives into deep water and hides under weeds.
> Some iguanas live in the desert and in Mexico.

Combining the first two sentences made for more effective writing. The fourth sentence in the original version made no particular sense in that location. Being there, it interrupted the flow of very specific detail about the life of an iguana. Note that the children chose to move that sentence to the end of the edited version, appropriately combining it with another sentence. The movement in the story now is from very specific details to less specific (some iguanas live in deserts, some in Mexico). The reconstruction of the sentences describing the ways the iguana reacts to danger is particularly interesting. The cognitive disorganization in the fifth sentence (original version) is eliminated in the revised version.

The work of these children shows very admirable progress toward increasingly sophisticated editing skills. Other groups may not progress as rapidly, or they may develop editing skills earlier. A sequence of developmental levels has not been established simply because so few teachers work consciously to develop these skills. The only generalization that can be made with some certainty is that by the time children are in the intermediate grades they should be able to deal effectively with such editing questions.

WHAT SHOULD BE RESHAPED?

The teacher whose children wrote the stories included above showed a rare understanding of the answer to a second important question: How much writing should be reshaped? It is crucial to keep in mind that, while all writing *can* be edited, not all writing *should* be edited. Much discretion is needed as the teacher decides how much editing children should be asked to do. If handled properly, the idea can be introduced, as this first grade teacher did, in a very pleasant, nonthreatening manner. Children found the questions she asked an interesting challenge. They thought about what they had written and produced better, more interesting writing as a result of the experience. With older children teachers need the same discretion. Reshaping writing must not become an onerous task. Sometimes teachers may ask editing questions with determination; at other times, sensing children are becoming discouraged with the process, they will not ask them to edit at all. How much reshaping is to be done cannot be answered apart from a particular group of children at a given time. Teachers must learn how to make such decisions in response to their own classrooms.

EDITING WITH OLDER CHILDREN

Until this point we have been talking about helping groups of children edit their stories. However, sometimes during the middle primary grades, teachers may sense that children have developed enough confidence in their ability to compose to be ready for help with individual editing. Having first done the process in a group will prepare the children to look at their own writing for ways in which it could be improved.

Older children can be helped to look analytically at their writing. Sample questions have been included to help children think about characterization (chapter three, page 96), setting (chapter four, page 118), and plot (chapter five, pages 168–169). In addition to these three major elements in writing, there are other aspects to be considered.

Central to effective composition is the ability to create *conversation* where appropriate. With younger children the teacher will simply note the presence or absence of conversation. In lower grades children can begin to write simple one to four word conversations. After much encouragement to write conversation, the teacher should help children consider more sophisticated questions:

- Does the conversation fit into the flow of the story? Does it seem forced or natural?

- Does the conversation show us something about the person? Can we learn something about what the character is like through what he/she says? [8]
- Is the conversation typical of the age of the character? If a young child is speaking, does it sound like a child? If a grandmother, does it sound like an older person? Grandmothers, for example, seldom say "Gee" or "neat."
- Is there some speech pattern that distinguishes one character from another? Even if a story is about two characters of the same age, is there some way their conversation sets them apart? This might be through recurrent vocabulary items or through sentence construction.

Related to these questions about conversation is the idea of dialect that reflects a particular location. In preparation we should share many stories with children that contain dialect conversation. We may read such stories as *Strawberry Girl* [9] for the Florida "cracker" dialect it contains and *Thee, Hannah* [10] for the Pennsylvania "plain-people" dialect it contains. Reading and consequent discussion of the dialects lays a groundwork for dialect writing, should children choose to use it.

In discussion the teacher will draw children's attention to how the dialect is similar to and different from the dialect the children speak. Children's ears can become very attuned to dialect differences, and they should be encouraged to try their hand at incorporating dialect into stories they write when it is appropriate.

Children can be helped to understand that evocation of

[8] This is an important question to consider because most children *tell* in direct narrative about characters rather than *show* about characters through conversation.

[9] Lois Lenski, *Strawberry Girl.*

[10] Marguerite De Angeli, *Thee, Hannah.*

mood may be achieved in a variety of ways. For elementary children it is usually achieved through word choice. Mood is thus related to description, either of the setting or of the people involved. Helping children choose adjectives that describe setting and people can strengthen a sense of mood in their writing.

One beginning activity to heighten awareness, in which children are asked to list all the adjectives that describe their classroom, was described in chapter four. A similar experience of searching for sensory words that convey mood is appropriate for describing almost any location. To develop mood, the teacher will help children move beyond simple descriptive words about how a location appears to the senses to a description of how it makes the child feel. Getting at feeling words is a first step toward the development of mood in writing.

In describing people, the teacher's goal is to help children see that particular word choices may help establish mood. We can, for example, describe a character as *fat*. Slightly different impressions are created, however, as we choose among other possibilities: *portly, pudgy, stout, corpulent, plump, chubby,* or *obese*. As the teacher and the children explore new words and their meanings, children are led to an understanding of the importance of well-chosen words and the different moods they can convey.

Another way mood is set is through the use of verbs. Children can be helped to see that the way a character *says* something can establish mood. A simple classroom exercise is to have children make a group list of all the other words one can use instead of *said*. One classroom teacher who tried this found that her children came up with 104 other possibilities to use instead of the pallid *said*.[11] In this context

[11] Included in J. W. Suber, *Guide to Teaching in the Elementary Language Arts*, p. 43.

you might share with children some of the old "Tom Swift" books, which Lake recommends as an excellent source of alternative ways to *say* something.[12] Searching for alternatives to the verb *walk* can also help children see how crucial word choice is in the establishment of mood. A child sent to the office may indeed walk there. Saying that he *straggled* to the office helps set the mood of apprehension about what may happen there more effectively than the word *walk*.

Conscious attention to the *climax* of a story is also necessary. Many teachers have had the experience of reading along in an interesting story written by a child, only to have it come abruptly to a conclusion as the child tacks on an arbitrary "The End." This is often due in large part to simple physical considerations. The child has written to get his or her ideas on paper, but stopped simply because he or she had more ideas than physical energy to write them down. The suggestions contained in chapter two for alternative ways to record compositions may well be extended into the intermediate grades if children seem to be using arbitrary endings without a real climax. The teacher wants to help young children consider: Does something exciting happen at the end? With older children we move from a simple quantitative question: Is a climax included? to a more qualitative question: Is what happens at the climax logical within the context of the story?

Another consideration related to climax and conclusion is the nature of these. Because of the pervasive influence of television, children may have the idea that all stories must end happily. Indeed, movies also perpetuate this mistaken idea. Part of maturity in writing lies in the understanding that stories do not necessarily need to end happily. To encourage children to feel free to write a neutral or unhappy

[12] Mary Louise Lake, "First Aid for Vocabularies," *Elementary English*, November 1967, pp. 783–84.

ending to a story, teachers must provide them with models in literature. We might read *The Jazz Man* [13] in which the ending is, if not unhappy, at least uncertain. Or try sharing *Sounds of Sunshine, Sounds of Rain*,[14] another book in which the happy-ever-after syndrome is avoided. The teacher does not necessarily encourage or expect children to write a story with a neutral or unhappy ending. It is the teacher's responsibility, however, to show children that such an ending is an acceptable option, should the writer choose to exercise it. Older children know that in life things don't always work out happily, and they should be allowed to end a story in a variety of ways.

EDITING: A SLOWLY DEVELOPING ABILITY

The comments made in this chapter and the evaluation questions concluding previous chapters must be seen in a time context and a personality context. As teachers ask editing questions and try to help children evaluate the effectiveness of their own work, it is important that they remember this ability is slow to develop. Looking at one's own work is never easy; it is perhaps even more difficult for children than for adults. So teachers must work patiently, helping children edit some compositions, allowing them to simply write and enjoy others. By the time children leave elementary school, they should be able to deal with these suggested questions and others related to their work. In addition to a time context, there is also a personality context to consider.

The process of editing will be easier for some children than for others; some may simply never be able to look critically at their own writing. Something in the personality of chil-

---

[13] Mary H. Weik, *The Jazz Man*.
[14] Florence Parry Heide, *Sounds of Sunshine, Sounds of Rain*.

dren, perhaps a factor of psychological self-confidence, makes it possible to some children to deal easily with the kind of evaluation and editing suggested here. Other children are, and perhaps will always remain, so emotionally tied to what they have composed that to evaluate it and then edit it, is distasteful. Teachers must thus use discretion in how much editing they require of individual children. In this area, as in several other aspects of this program, teacher decision making will dictate the final shape of the writing curriculum.

What you have read is summary, outline, and forecast. It is a summary of what a group of teachers interested in writing did in implementing a composition curriculum. It is an outline of a sequentially organized writing program designed to produce better writers and writing. Finally, it is a forecast of what you, a classroom teacher, can do with your children to help them develop skill in writing. Writing is only one way of communicating, yet it can be a very powerful way of sharing ideas if we can help children develop the ability to share their thoughts through the written word.

BIBLIOGRAPHY

BOOKS AND PERIODICALS

Adoff, Arnold, ed. *Black Out Loud*. New York: The Macmillan Co., 1970.

Alexander, Lloyd. *The King's Fountain*. New York: E. P. Dutton and Co., 1971.

Anderson, Jean M., and Kahler, Martha. "It's Raining Cats and Dogs." *Instructor*, January 1971, pp. 69–70.

Applegate, Mauree. *When the Teacher Says, "Write a Poem."* New York: Harper and Row Publishers, 1965.

————. *When the Teacher Says, "Write a Story."* New York: Harper and Row Publishers, 1965.

Arbuthnot, May Hill. *Arbuthnot Anthology of Children's Literature*. Glenview, Ill.: Scott, Foresman and Co., 1971.

Armstrong, William. *Sounder*. New York: Harper and Row Publishers, 1969.

Arnstein, Flora J. *Poetry and the Child*. New York: Dover Publications, 1962.

Atwater, Richard, and Atwater, Florence. *Mr. Popper's Penguins*. Boston: Little, Brown and Co., 1938.

Austin, Mary C., and Mills, Queenie B., eds. *The Sound of Poetry*. Boston: Allyn and Bacon, 1967.

Bailey, Carolyn S. *Miss Hickory*. New York: The Viking Press, 1946.

Barron, Frank X., *Creative Person and Creative Process*. New York: Holt, Rinehart and Winston, 1969.

Behn, Harry, trans. *Cricket Songs*. New York: Harcourt, Brace and World, 1964.

———. *The Golden Hive*. New York: Harcourt, Brace and World, 1966.

———. *The Wizard in the Well*. New York: Harcourt, Brace and World, 1956.

Belting, Natalie. *The Sun Is a Golden Earring*. New York: Holt, Rinehart and Winston, 1962.

Berg, Jean Horton. *Miss Tessie Tate*. Philadelphia: The Westminster Press, 1967.

Blake, Howard E. "Written Composition in English Primary Schools." *Elementary English,* October 1971, pp. 605–16.

Blume, Judy. *Are You There, God? It's Me, Margaret*. New York: Dell Publishing Co., 1970.

Borten, Helen. *Do You See What I See?* New York: Abelard-Schuman, 1959.

———. *A Picture Has a Special Look*. New York: Abelard-Schuman, 1961.

Brown, Marcia. *The Bun*. New York: Harcourt Brace Jovanovich, 1972.

Burns, Paul C., et al. "Written Composition." In *The Language Arts in Childhood Education*. Chicago: Rand McNally and Co., 1971.

Burrows, Alvina T., et al. *They All Want to Write*. New York: Holt, Rinehart and Winston, 1964.

Burrows, Alvina T.; Monson, Dianne L.; and Stauffer, Russell G. *New Horizons in the Language Arts*. New York: Harper and Row Publishers, 1972.

Burton, Virginia L. *The Emperor's New Clothes*. Boston: Houghton Mifflin Co., 1949.

Carlson, Ruth Kearney. *Sparkling Words*. Geneva, Ill.: Paladin House Publishers, 1973.

Cassedy, Sylvia, and Suetake, Kunihiro. *Birds, Frogs, and Moonlight*. Garden City, N.Y.: Doubleday and Co., 1967.

Cataldo, John. *Words and Calligraphy for Children*. New York: Reinhold Book Corp., 1969.

Caudill, Rebecca. *Did You Carry the Flag Today, Charley?* New York: Holt, Rinehart and Winston, 1966.

Clark, Ann Nolan. *Secret of the Andes*. New York: The Viking Press, 1952.

Clegg, A. B. *The Excitement of Writing.* New York: Schocken Books, 1972.

Coatsworth, Elizabeth. *Lonely Maria.* New York: Pantheon Books, 1960.

Cohen, Miriam. *Will I Have a Friend?* New York: The Macmillan Co., 1967.

Cole, William, ed. *Beastly Boys and Ghastly Girls.* Cleveland: World Publishing Co., 1971.

Corbin, Richard. *The Teaching of Writing in Our Schools.* New York: The Macmillan Co., 1966.

Cornish, Sam, and Dixon, Lucian, eds. *Chicory: Young Voices from the Black Ghetto.* New York: Association Press, 1969.

Craig, M. Jean. *What Did You Dream?* New York: Abelard-Schuman, 1964.

Crosby, Muriel (ed.). *The World of Language.* 9 vols. Chicago: Follett Educational Corp., 1970.

Curriculum for English, A, book 4. Lincoln, Neb.: The University of Nebraska Press, 1966.

Dahl, Roald. *Charlie and the Chocolate Factory.* New York: Alfred A. Knopf, 1964.

Dalgliesh, Alice. *The Bears on Hemlock Mountain.* New York: Charles Scribner's Sons, 1952.

Davis, David C., et al. *Playway: Education for Reality.* Minneapolis: Winston Press, 1973.

De Angeli, Marguerite. *The Door in the Wall.* Garden City, N.Y.: Doubleday and Co., 1949.

————. *Henner's Lydia.* Garden City, N.Y.: Doubleday Doran and Co. 1936.

————. *Jared's Island.* Garden City, N.Y.: Doubleday and Co., 1947.

————. *Petite Suzanne.* Garden City, N.Y.: Doubleday, Doran and Co., 1937.

————. *Thee, Hannah.* Garden City, N.Y.: Doubleday, Doran and Co., 1940.

————. *Yonnie Wondernose.* Garden City, N.Y.: Doubleday and Co., 1944.

Dearmin, Jennie T. "Teaching Your Children to Paint Pictures with Words." *Grade Teacher,* March 1965, pp. 26–27.

Dechant, Emerald V. *Improving the Teaching of Reading.* Englewood Cliffs, N.J.: Prentice-Hall, 1970.

Donoghue, Mildred R. *The Child and the English Language Arts.* Dubuque, Iowa: William C. Brown Co., 1971.

Donovan, John. *I'll Get There. It Better Be Worth the Trip.* New York: Dell Publishing Co., 1969.

Dunning, Stephen, et al., eds. *Reflections on a Gift of Watermelon Pickle . . .* Glenview, Ill.: Scott, Foresman and Co., 1966.

————. *Some Haystacks Don't Even Have Any Needle.* Glenview, Ill.: Scott, Foresman and Co., 1969.

Durham, John. *Me and Arch and the Pest.* New York: The Four Winds Press, 1970.

Edmund, Neal R. "Do Intermediate Grade Pupils Write About Their Problems?" *Elementary English* 37 (April 1960) : 242–43.

Ellentuck, Shan. *A Sunflower as Big as the Sun.* Garden City, N.Y.: Doubleday and Co., 1968.

Engdahl, Sylvia L. *Enchantress from the Stars.* New York: Atheneum Publishers, 1971.

Enright, Elizabeth. *Gone Away Lake.* New York: Harcourt, Brace and Co., 1957.

————. *The Saturdays.* New York: Rinehart and Co., 1941.

————. *Then There Were Five.* New York: Holt, Rinehart and Winston, 1944.

————. *Thimble Summer.* New York: Rinehart and Co., 1938.

Estes, Eleanor. *The Hundred Dresses.* New York: Harcourt, Brace and Co., 1944.

————. *Rufus M.* New York: Harcourt, Brace and Co., 1943.

Evans, Robert. "A Glove Thrown Down." *Elementary English*, May 1967, pp. 523–27.

Evertts, Eldonna. "Dinosaurs, Witches, and Anti-Aircraft: Primary Composition." In *Language and the Language Arts*, edited by Johanna S. DeStefano and Sharon E. Fox. Boston: Little, Brown and Co., 1974.

Fillmer, H. Thompson, et al. *Patterns of Language.* 8 vols. New York: American Book Co., 1974.

Fisher, Aileen. *Cricket in a Thicket.* New York: Charles Scribner's Sons, 1963.

Fitzhugh, Louise. *The Long Secret.* New York: Dell Publishing Co., 1965.

Flack, Marjorie. *Walter, the Lazy Mouse.* Garden City, N.Y.: Doubleday, Doran and Co., 1937.

Fleischman, Sid. *Longbeard the Wizard.* Boston: Little, Brown and Co., 1970.

Flora, James. *Leopold, the see-through crumpicker.* New York: Harcourt, Brace and World, 1961.

Folta, Bernarr. *Three Strategies for Revising Sentences.* Terre Haute, Ind.: Indiana Council of Teachers of English, n.d.

Forman, James. *The Traitors.* New York: Farrar, Straus and Giroux, 1968.

Forsman, Bettie. *From Lupita's Hill.* New York: Atheneum Publishers, 1973.

Foster, Genevieve. *Abraham Lincoln.* New York: Charles Schribner's Sons, 1950.

Fournier, Raymond. *Thinking and Writing: An Inductive Program in Composition.* Englewood Cliffs, N.J.: Prentice-Hall, 1969.

Fox, Edward S. *Massacre Inlet.* Garden City, N.Y.: Doubleday and Co., 1965.

Fox, Paula. *A Likely Place.* New York: The Macmillan Co., 1967.

———. *The Slave Dancer.* Scarsdale, N.Y.: Bradbury Press, 1973.

Gaeddert, Lou Ann. *Noisy Nancy Norris.* Garden City, N.Y.: Doubleday and Co., 1971.

Gag, Wanda. *Gone Is Gone.* New York: Coward-McCann, 1935.

———, ed. and trans. *More Tales from Grimm.* New York: Coward-McCann, 1947.

Galdone, Paul. *Three Aesop Fox Fables.* New York: The Seabury Press, 1971.

Gardner, Martin, ed. *The Annotated Alice.* New York: Bramhall House, 1960.

Gates, Doris. *Blue Willow.* New York: The Viking Press, 1948.

Godden, Rumer. *Impunity Jane.* New York: The Viking Press, 1954.

———. *Mouse House.* New York: The Viking Press, 1957.

———. *The Mousewife.* New York: The Viking Press, 1951.

Goudge, Elizabeth. *Linnets and Valerians.* New York: Coward-McCann, 1964.

Grahame, Kenneth. *The Wind in the Willows.* New York: Scribner's, 1908.

Greene, Constance C. *A Girl Called Al.* New York: The Viking Press, 1969.

Greene, Harry A., and Petty, Walter T. *Developing Language Skills in the Elementary Schools.* Boston: Allyn and Bacon, 1971.

Grimm, Jacob Ludwig Carl, and Grimm, Wilhelm Carl. *Grimm's Fairy Tales.* New York: The Viking Press, 1973.

Hall, Adelaide. *The Enormous Sweater.* New York: Lothrop, Lee and Shepard, 1966.

Hand, John S., et al. *Progress in English.* 10 vols. Palo Alto, Calif.: Laidlaw Brothers, 1972.

Harris, Christie. *Confessions of a Toe-Hanger.* New York: Atheneum Publishers, 1967.

Hartley, Ruth. "Poetry for Boys in Primary Grades." *Elementary English,* December 1972, pp. 1153–57.

Haugaard, E. C. *Hans Christian Andersen—The Complete Fairy Tales and Stories.* Garden City, N.Y.: Doubleday and Co., 1974.

Haviland, Virginia. *Favorite Fairy Tales Told in Scotland.* Boston: Little, Brown and Co., 1963.

Heide, Florence Parry. *The Key.* New York: Atheneum Publishers, 1972.

———. *Sounds of Sunshine, Sounds of Rain.* New York: Parents Magazine Press, 1970.

Henderson, Harold. *Haiku in English.* Champaign, Ill.: National Council of Teachers of English, 1967.

———. *An Introduction to Haiku.* Garden City, N.Y.: Doubleday and Co., 1958.

Henry, Marguerite. *Justin Morgan Had a Horse.* Chicago: Rand McNally and Co., 1971.

Hogrogian, Nancy. *The Renowned History of Little Red Riding Hood.* New York: Thomas Y. Crowell Co., 1967.

Holman, Felice. *The Cricket Winter.* New York: W. W. Norton and Co., 1967.

Hopkins, Lee Bennett, comp. *City Talk.* New York: Alfred A. Knopf, 1970.

———. "For Creative Fun, Let Them Try a Cinquain." *Grade Teacher,* December 1966, pp. 83ff.

———. "From Trudeau's Garden." *Elementary English,* October 1967, pp. 613–14.

Huber, Miriam Blanton. *Story and Verse for Children.* New York: The Macmillan Co., 1965.

Huffard, Grace, et. al., eds. *My Poetry Book.* New York: Henry Holt and Co., 1956.

Hutchinson, Veronica S. *Chimney Corner Fairy Tales.* New York: Minton Balch, 1926.

Ireson, Barbara. *The Gingerbread Man.* New York: W. W. Norton and Co., 1963.

Irwin, Betty K. *Behind the Magic Line.* Boston: Little, Brown and Co., 1969.

Jarrell, Randall. *The Bat Poet.* New York: The Macmillan Co., 1964.

———, trans. *Snow-white and the Seven Dwarfs.* New York: Farrar, Straus and Giroux, 1972.

Johnson, Edna, et al. *Anthology of Children's Literature*. Boston: Houghton Mifflin Co., 1970.

Johnson, Elizabeth. *Stuck with Luck*. Boston: Little, Brown and Co., 1967.

Joseph, Stephen M. *The Me Nobody Knows*. New York: Avon Books, 1969.

Judson, Clara Ingram. *Abraham Lincoln*. Chicago: Follett Publishing Co., 1950.

Kirby, Anne. *Elementary School English*. 6 vols. Palo Alto, Calif.: Addison-Wesley, 1967.

Koch, Kenneth. *Wishes, Lies and Dreams*. New York: Vintage Books, 1970.

Konigsburg, E. L. *Jennifer, Hecate, Macbeth, William McKinley, and Me, Elizabeth*. New York: Atheneum Publishers, 1967.

Krumgold, Joseph. *Onion John*. New York: Thomas Y. Crowell Co., 1959.

Lake, Mary Louise. "First Aid for Vocabularies." *Elementary English*, November 1967, pp. 783–84.

Landrum, Roger. *A Day Dream I Had at Night*. New York: Teachers and Writers Collaborative, 1971.

Langdon, Margaret. *Let the Children Write*. London: Longmans, Green and Co., 1961.

Larrick, Nancy. *Green Is Like a Meadow of Grass*. Champaign, Ill.: Garrard Publishing Co., 1968.

Lenski, Lois. *Cotton in My Sack*. Philadelphia: J. B. Lippincott Co., 1945.

———. *Judy's Journey*. Philadelphia: J. B. Lippincott Co., 1947.

———. *Strawberry Girl*. Philadelphia: J. B. Lippincott Co., 1945.

Lewis, C. S. *The Lion, the Witch and the Wardrobe*. New York: The Macmillan Co., 1961.

Lewis, Richard, ed. *In a Spring Garden*. New York: The Dial Press, 1965.

———, comp. *Miracles*. New York: Simon and Schuster, 1966.

———, comp. *The Wind and the Rain*. New York: Simon and Schuster, 1968.

Lionni, Leo. *Swimmy*. New York: Pantheon Books, 1963.

———. *Theodore and the Talking Mushroom*. New York: Panetheon Books, 1971.

Livingston, Myra Cohn. *The Malibu and Other Poems*. New York: Atheneum Publishers, 1972.

Lobel, Arnold. *Giant John.* New York: Harper and Row Publishers, 1964.

Lytton, Hugh. *Creativity and Education.* New York: Schocken Books, 1972.

McCord, David. *Every Time I Climb a Tree.* Boston: Little, Brown and Co., 1971.

———. *For Me to Say.* Boston: Little, Brown and Co., 1970.

———. *Take Sky.* Boston: Little, Brown, 1962.

McDermott, Gerald, ed. *Anansi, the Spider.* New York: Holt, Rinehart and Winston, 1972.

Marshall, James. *What's the Matter with Carruthers?* Boston: Houghton Mifflin Co., 1972.

Marshall, Sybil. *An Experiment in Education.* Cambridge: The University Press, 1966.

Mason, Miriam E. *Caroline and Her Kettle Named Maud.* New York: The Macmillan Co., 1951.

Mayne, William. *Earthfasts.* New York: E. P. Dutton and Co., 1967.

Mearns, Hughes. *Creative Power: The Education of Youth in the Creative Arts.* 2d ed. New York: Dover Publications, 1958.

Merriam, Eve. *It Doesn't Always Have to Rhyme.* New York: Atheneum Publishers, 1964.

Miles, Miska. *Gertrude's Pocket.* Boston: Little, Brown and Co., 1970.

———. *Nobody's Cat.* Boston: Little, Brown and Co., 1969.

Miller, Edna. *Mouskin's Golden House.* Englewood Cliffs, N.J.: Prentice-Hall, 1964.

Milne, A. A. *Winnie the Pooh.* New York: E. P. Dutton and Co., 1926.

Mizumara, Kazue. *If I Were a Mother.* New York: Thomas Y. Crowell Co., 1968.

Montresor, Beni. *Cinderella.* New York: Alfred A. Knopf. 1965.

Mosel, Arlene. *The Funny Little Woman.* New York: E. P. Dutton and Co., 1972.

Nachbar, Cornelia, et al., *Flying Free,* American Language Today, vol. 6, New York: Webster Division, McGraw-Hill Book Co., 1974.

Neville, Emily C. *Berries Goodman.* New York: Harper and Row Publishers, 1965.

Ney, John. *Ox.* Boston: Little, Brown and Co., 1970.

Norton, Mary. *Bedknob and Broomstick.* New York: Harcourt, Brace and Co., 1957.

———. *The Borrowers.* New York: Harcourt, Brace and Co., 1953.

Norton, Natalie. *The Little Old Man.* Chicago: Rand McNally and Co., 1959.

Odland, Norine. *Teaching Literature in the Elementary School.* Champaign, Ill.: National Council of Teachers of English, 1969.

O'Neill, Mary. *Words Words Words.* Garden City, N.Y.: Doubleday and Co., 1966.

Palmer, Geoffrey, and Lloyd, Noel, eds. *Round About Eight.* London: Frederick Warne and Co., 1972.

Parkinson, Ethelyn M. *Never Go Anywhere with Digby.* Nashville, Tenn.: Abingdon Press, 1971.

Petty, Walter T., and Bowen, Mary E. *Slithery Snakes and Other Aids to Children's Writing.* New York: Meredith Corp., 1967.

Petty, Walter T., et al. *Experiences in Language.* Boston: Allyn and Bacon, 1973.

Pilon, A. Barbara. *Concrete Is Not Always Hard.* Middletown, Conn.: Xerox Educational Publications, 1972.

Pratt-Butler, Grace. *Let Them Write Creatively.* Columbus, Ohio: Charles E. Merrill Publishing Co., 1973.

Preston, Edna M. *Horrible Hepzibah.* New York: The Viking Press, 1971.

Read, Herbert. *This Way, Delight.* New York: Pantheon Books, 1956.

Reeves, James. *Blackbird in the Lilac.* New York: E. P. Dutton and Co., 1959.

Robertson, Jane E. "Figurative Language." *Instructor,* November 1973, pp. 50–51.

Robertson, Keith. *Henry Reed, Inc.* New York: The Viking Press, 1958.

Root, Shelton L. "What's Wrong with Reading Aloud?" *Elementary English,* December 1967, pp. 929–32.

Rosner, Stanley. *The Creative Experience.* New York: Grossman Publishers, 1970.

Sawyer, Ruth. *Journey Cake, Ho!* New York: The Viking Press, 1953.

Schiller, Andrew et al. *Language and How to Use It.* 9 vols. Glenview, Ill.: Scott, Foresman and Co., 1969.

Schwalje, Marjory. *Mr. Angelo.* New York: Abelard-Schuman, 1960.

Scott, Ann Herbert. *Sam.* New York: McGraw-Hill Book Co., 1967.

Segal, Lore. *Tell Me a Mitzi.* New York: Farrar, Straus and Giroux, 1970.

Sharmat, Marjorie W. *Getting Something on Maggie Marmelstein.* New York: Harper and Row Publishers, 1971.

Smith, James A., *Creative Teaching of the Language Arts in the Elementary School.* 2d ed. Boston: Allyn and Bacon, 1973.

Snyder, Zilpha Keatley. *Eyes in the Fishbowl.* New York: Atheneum Publishers, 1968.

Starbird, Kaye. *A Snail's a Failure Socially.* Philadelphia: J. B. Lippincott Co., 1966.

Stewig, John Warren. *Exploring Language with Children.* Columbus, Ohio: Charles E. Merrill Publishing Co., 1974.

————. "Metaphor and Children's Writing." *Elementary English,* February 1966, pp. 121–23.

————. *Spontaneous Drama: A Language Art.* Columbus, Ohio: Charles E. Merrill Publishing Co., 1973.

Strickland, Ruth G. *The Language Arts in the Elementary School.* Lexington, Mass.: D. C. Heath and Co., 1969.

Suber, J. W. *Guide to Teaching in the Elementary Language Arts.* Charlotte, N.C.: Charlotte-Mecklenburg Public Schools, 1966.

Thompson, Kay. *Eloise.* New York: Simon and Schuster, 1955.

Thurber, James. *Many Moons.* New York: Harcourt, Brace and Co., 1943.

Tiedt, Iris M. "A New Poetry Form: The Diamante." *Elementary English,* May 1969, pp. 588–89.

Tolkien, J. R. R. *The Hobbit.* Boston: Houghton Mifflin Co., 1937.

Tresselt, Alvin. *Hide and Seek Fog.* New York: Lothrop, Lee and Shepard Co., 1965.

————. *White Snow, Bright Snow.* New York: Lothrop, Lee and Shepard Co., 1947.

Untermeyer, Louis. *Modern American Poetry.* New York: Harcourt Brace Jovanovich, 1950.

————, ed. *The Golden Book of Fun and Nonsense.* New York: Golden Press Publishers, 1970.

————, ed. *The Golden Treasury of Poetry.* New York: Golden Press Publishers, 1959.

Updike, John. *A Child's Calendar.* New York: Alfred A. Knopf, 1965.

Walter, Nina Willis. *Let Them Write Poetry.* New York: Holt, Rinehart and Winston, 1962.

Weik, Mary H. *The Jazz Man.* New York: Atheneum Publishers, 1966.

White, E. B. *Charlotte's Web.* New York: Harper and Brothers, 1952.

Whitehead, Robert. *Children's Literature: Strategies of Teaching.* Englewood Cliffs, N.J.: Prentice-Hall, 1968.

Wilde, Oscar. *The Selfish Giant.* Irvington-on-Hudson, N.Y.: The Harvey House, 1968.

Wilder, Laura Ingalls. *Little House in the Big Woods*. New York: Harper and Brothers, 1932.

————. "The Little House on the Prarie." In *A Curriculum for English*, bk. 4, pp. 89–100. Lincoln, Neb.: The University of Nebraska Press, 1966.

Wojciechowska, Maia. *Hey, What's Wrong With This One?* New York: Harper and Row Publishers, 1969.

Wolsch, Robert A. *Poetic Composition Through the Grades*. New York: Teachers College Press, 1970.

Yashima, Taro. *Crowboy*. New York: The Viking Press, 1955.

RECORDINGS AND FILMSTRIPS

Borten, Helen. *A Picture Has a Special Look*. Weston Woods (LTR-054). With filmstrip.

Developing Language Arts Skills. Chicago: The Society for Visual Education (L2-R).

Folk Tales from Indonesia. Folkways Records (FP 102).

Folk Tales from West Africa. Folkways Records (FP 103).

Grahame, Kenneth. *Wind in the Willows*. Pathways of Sound (POS 1022, 1026, 1029, and 1039).

Karloff, Boris, reader. *The Three Little Pigs and Other Fairy Tales*. Caedmon Records (TC 1129).

McCord, David, et al., readers. *Poetry Parade*. Weston Woods (703–704).

"Metaphors and Similes—Imagery!" In *What Is Poetry?*, no. 9. Caedmon Records (CFS-501). With filmstrip.

Nursery and Mother Goose Songs. Bowmar Records (B-115 LP).

Ritchard, Cyril, reader. *Alice in Wonderland*. Riverside Records (SDP 22).

————, et al., readers. *Mother Goose*. Caedmon Records (TC 1091).

Sandburg, Carl. *Poems for Children*. Caedmon Records (TC 1124).

————. *Rootabaga Stories*. Caedmon Records (TC 1089).

Sawyer, Ruth, reader. *Joy to the World*. Weston Woods (707).

————, reader. *Ruth Sawyer, Storyteller*. Weston Woods (701-702).

Schildkraut, Joseph, reader. *Grimm Fairy Tales*. Caedmon Records (TC 1062).

Simon, Paul, and Garfunkle, Art. *Sounds of Silence*. Columbia (CS 9269).

Wilde, Oscar. *The Selfish Giant*. Weston Woods (SF 132), With filmstrip.

INDEX